A Single Hand
Cannot Applaud

The value of using the book of Proverbs
in sharing the Gospel with Muslims

Bert de Ruiter

Bibliographic information published by the Deutsche Nationalbibliothek
The Deutsche Nationalbibliothek lists this publication in the Deutsche
Nationalbibliografie; detailed bibliographic data are available in the Internet
at http://dnb.d-nb.de.

ISBN 978-3-941750-07-4

VTR Publications
Gogolstr. 33, 90475 Nürnberg, Germany
http://www.vtr-online.eu

© 2011 by Bert de Ruiter

Printed by Lightning Source (UK/USA)

Contents

Introduction

With about 1.5 billion adherents, which is a little over one fifth of the world's population, Islam is the second largest religion in the world. When Jesus gave His followers the so-called Great Commission, He commanded us "to make disciples of all nations, baptizing them in the name of the Father, and of the Son and of the Holy Spirit, and teaching them to obey everything I have commanded you" (Matthew 28:19, 20).

From this and other verses in the Bible and from the fact that the Bible portrays our Heavenly Father as a 'missionary God', it is clear that God wants us to make disciples among the Muslims. It is necessary that the church of God reaches out to the Muslims with the Gospel of Jesus Christ and invite them to put their thrust in Him for their eternal salvation.

Necessity and Relevance

Since the 6th Century A.D., when Islam came into existence, the relationship between Christians and Muslims has often been difficult and full of tensions. It might be for this reason that for many centuries, the church by and large ignored the Muslim countries when it came to carry out the Great Commission. As recently as the 1970s, only 2 percent of Christian mission groups had staff working among Muslims[1]. Although that number has shot up in recent years, with more than 27,000 missionaries placed amid Muslims by 2001,[2] this still means that only about 10% of all missionaries work among Muslims.

But the 'success rate' has been quite low. Of course, Muslims have come to Christ, sometimes even in large numbers (e.g. in the past 2 years 50.000 Iranians have accepted Christ[3] and the church in Algeria has grown to about 7.000 Kabyle Christians,[4] but overall, we can say that Muslims have not been

---

[1]   Kevin Greeson, http://www.religionnewsblog.com/ (accessed March 17,2005).

[2]   Ibid.

[3]   *International Antioch Ministries*, June 14, 2004, "Press Release," http://iam-online.net/Press_release_PDFs/IAMTVrelease_Final.com%20(Read-Only).pdf. (accessed February 20, 2006).

[4]   *The 30-Days Prayer Network*, "The Amazing Story of Christianity in Algeria," http://www.30-days.net/muslims/muslims-in/north-african/algeria-kabyles. (accessed August, 2010).

very responsive. One of the reasons for this might be that Islam in its theology has embraced so much of Christianity that it has become immune for it. This is particularly true when we look at the Scriptures.

Christians, who want to share about God with their Muslim friends, understandably try to have Muslims read the Bible. The Bible is the Word of God, in which God reveals the eternal truth. Instead of giving Muslims the whole Bible from the start, many prefer to give them one of the Gospels, particularly the Gospel of Luke or John. Giving a Gospel to a Muslims who expresses interest in the Christian faith is worthwhile. The Gospels can be used as a tool to introduce Muslims to the life and ministry of Jesus Christ.

Islam doesn't deny the fact that God gave a book to his prophet Moses (Torah); David (the Psalms); Jesus (Gospel), but many Muslims believe that the followers of these people have corrupted these books. That perception is one of the reasons why Muslims find it difficult to read the Bible. Many are convinced that all they need to know about the Bible, they can find in their book, the Qur'an. Many Muslims believe that their Holy Book, the Qur'an, supersedes the Bible and that because the Books of God as revealed to Moses and Jesus do not exist now in the original form and language, the Bible contains only parts of the original words of God. They believe that one of the functions of the Qur'an is to confirm the truth that is left in the older scriptures, even after many interpolations and revisions have affected substantial changes in them.

The Qur'anic position about the previous scriptures is clarified in the following verse:

> To thee We sent the Scripture in truth, confirming the scripture that came before it, and guarding it in safety: so judge between them by what God hath revealed, and follow not their vain desires, diverging from the Truth that hath come to thee. To each among you have we prescribed a law and an open way. If God had so willed, He would have made you a single people, but (His plan is) to test you in what He hath given you: so strive as in a race in all virtues. The goal of you all is to God; it is He that will show you the truth of the matters in which ye dispute (Surah 5:48).[5]

This verse is interpreted to mean that the Qur'an confirms the truth that remains in the former scriptures. That the keepers of the previous books had distorted them is made deducted from another verse: "Then woe to those who write the Book with their own hands, and then say: 'This is from God,' to traf-

---

[5]   Abdullah Yusuf Ali, *The Holy Qur'an: English Text and Translation* (Kuala Lumpur: Islamic Book Trust, 2003).

fic with it for miserable price! – Woe to them for what their hands do write, and for the gain they make thereby" (Surah 2:79).

Lamaan Ball, editor of *Ask About Islam*, writes:

> We are told in the Qur'an only to verify that what is in the Qur'an agrees with some extant verses of the Bible. The Muslims can quote the Bible, because they believe there is some truth in it. But we need to be clear: we understand that there is also falsehood there, which is wrongly presented as truth. By quoting the Bible we can show that the Qur'an confirms teachings already present in he earlier books. We must however always be clear that we are not asserting anything else about the remaining contents of those earlier books.[6]

Given this antagonism among a large percentage of Muslims toward Christianity in general and the Bible in particular, there might be a need to prepare the ground before a Muslim can be persuaded to read the Bible.

To stimulate a Muslim to read the Scriptures, we need to find common ground between their world view and the Bible. Can it be that of all the sixty-six books of the Bible, we find such common ground in the book of Proverbs?

The universal character of the book of Proverbs seems to make the book a useful bridge between the truth of the God and those outside the Christian faith, including Muslims. The book of Proverbs is part of the Wisdom books in the Bible and according to Beardslee, "in the Hebraic and Jewish world wisdom served of building a bridge between the perspective of faith and the experience of men outside the circle of faith."[7]

Another reason why the book could be a useful tool for sharing the truth of God with Muslims is that some of the verses clearly come from foreign soil. They might find some of their own truth in the Book of Proverbs.

Also, as will be pointed out in chapter 1, the respect for wisdom that many Arab and Berber culture have helps explain the frequency of proverb use in their culture. It has been said that "Arabs make more use of proverbs than

---

[6] Lamaan Ball, "What Islam Says About The Bible," *Ask About Islam*, July 6, 2002, www.islamonline.net/servlet/Satellit?pagename=IslamOnline-English-AAbout Islam/AskAboutIslamE/AskAboutIslamE&cid=1123996015484/ (accessed February 20, 2006).

[7] William Beardslee, "Uses of the Proverb in the Synoptic Gospel," in The Wisdom of Many: essays on the proverb, ed. Wolfgang Mieder & Alan Dundes (New York: Garland, 1981), 162.

most other nations in the world."[8] They take vast pride in being able to invoke proverbs when the need arises and pay great respect to any person who is capable of using these sayings correctly.

God's wisdom found in the book of Proverbs seems to resemble the content of proverbial sayings in many Muslim cultures. It is therefore very likely that using this book as a tool in sharing the Word of God with Muslims can create openings where there were none.

Muslims are familiar with Solomon of Scripture because he is mentioned in the Qur'an,[9] but most have never read his words. The wisdom God gave Solomon might be a natural link to Muslim people so they can come to know more about God.

Purpose of this Book

To demonstrate whether, and if so, in what way, the book of Proverbs can be like a *plow* to soften the hearts of Muslims for the Word of God and a *bridge* to introduce them to the Good News of Jesus Christ.

Objectives

In order to accomplish the purpose mentioned this book has the following objectives:

1. To investigate the role of proverbs in Arab culture. Chapter one provides a discussion of the role and influence of proverbs in Arab culture in general and Moroccan culture in particular.

2. To make sense of the book of Proverbs. Chapter two discusses the structure, content and theology of the book of Proverbs.

4. To do a comparative study between Moroccan proverbs and the book of Proverbs. Chapter three lists more than hundred Moroccan proverbs and compares them with verses of the book of Proverbs.

5. To compose a Gospel presentation based on the book of Proverbs. Chapter four discusses the question how we can share the Gospel with our Muslim

---

[8]   Sheila K. Webster, "Arabic Proverbs and Related Forms," in *Proverbium: Yearbook of International Proverb Scholarship* (Burlington, Vermont: University of Vermont, 1986), 180.

[9]   The Qur'an identifies Solomon as a prophet to whom God gave great knowledge, wealth and superior wisdom. The Qur'an speaks about Solomon's glorious kingdom, his mighty army and his superior morality. (see Soera 6:83-87; 21:78-82; 27:15-44; 34:12-14; 38:30-44)

friend, using the book of Proverbs, particularly through linking the person of Jesus Christ with the content and theology of the book of Proverbs.

6. To survey the experiences of Christians in using proverbs and the book of Proverbs in their contact with Muslims. Chapter five gives examples of Christians that have used indigenous proverbs and/or the book of Proverbs to share the Gospel of Jesus Christ.

7. To recommend how to best make use of the Book of Proverbs as a pre-evangelism tool. Chapter six summaries the main points of the previous chapters and comes up with guidelines and recommendations for the use of the book of Proverbs in evangelizing Muslims.

Terminology

I will use both verses from the biblical book of Proverbs (which I will refer to as 'Proverbs' or 'the book of Proverbs') as well as proverbial sayings that are common in Moroccan culture (which I will call 'proverbs' or 'Moroccan proverbs').

I will use the term 'Arab' and its related forms several times. In doing so I am aware of the fact that the content of this word is used differently by a variety of people. With many others I consider the countries in North Africa and the Middle East that are part of 'The Arab League' and where Arabic is the main national language, Arab nations. But this doesn't mean that all citizens can be called Arabs. In Morocco, which will be the main Arab country discussed in this book, we find peoples that, although they speak Arabic, do not consider themselves Arabs. Many of the citizens of Morocco are Berbers, whose ancestors are the origin inhabitants of the region before the Arab armies invaded their countries in the 7th Century AD and following. Many of the Moroccans that have settled in the Netherlands are of Berber background and would be offended when being addressed as Arabs. Most of them speak Arabic, but their heart language is one of the Berber (Amazigh) languages. When possible, I will differentiate between the Arabic proverbs and proverbs that originated in the Berber culture.

Delimitations

Although I have referred to Muslims in general thus far in this introduction, the content of this book particularly deals with Moroccan Muslims.

Having said this I hope that it will be useful for those ministering to Muslims of other cultural and linguistic background and living in other parts of the world. I believe that some of the principles mentioned can be applied to Muslims in general, as will be pointed out in chapter six, where I will look at lessons to be learned from the use of Proverbs in ministering to Muslims.

In chapter two I will touch on the background and theology of Proverbs, but it is beyond the scope of this study to address all aspects of the controversial issues related to this book, particularly regarding authorship and date and its place in the Bible. I believe that Solomon is the author/compiler of the book of Proverbs and that the book is part of God's revelation to humankind and that its theology is fully in accordance with what God has revealed about Himself, humankind and the way He wants us to live, throughout the whole Bible.

Because I don't speak any of the main languages of Morocco (Arabic, Berber or French), I have been working with English, German and Dutch translations of the proverbs that are used in this study. This has limited the depth of this book, because it prevented me from reading useful books and articles in Arabic, Berber and French and also it hindered my communication with Moroccans that would have liked to be good resource people. Also there are many more proverbs that I could have used, but these are not translated in one of the languages that I'm familiar with.

Methodology

The content of this book is based on information obtained through books, articles, electronic media, unpublished materials, correspondence and interaction with various people, including colleagues serving among Muslims and several of my Moroccan friends.

Conclusion

Opening the hearts of Muslims for the truth of the Gospel and the glory of God in Christ is the work of the Sovereign God by His Holy Spirit. There is no success formula to accomplish this. On the other hand, servants of the Lord should not be blind to the tools that the Lord provides us to accomplish His work in the hearts of Muslims. This study wants to pursue whether the book of Proverbs could be such a tool and if so, in what way.

Chapter 1

The Role of Proverbs in Arab Culture

This chapter clarifies what role proverbs play in the culture of the Arab world in general and of Morocco in particular.

What is Meant by a Proverb?

Before proceeding in explaining the role of proverbs in Arabic and Moroccan society, it is useful to clarify what is meant by a proverb. Lord John Russell, an English statesman, defined a proverb by saying it is "one man's wit and all men's wisdom."[10] Thompson believes this definition points to three very common features of proverbial lore:

1. An arresting and individually inspired form ('wit of one')
2. A wide appeal and endorsement ('of many')
3. A content which commends itself to the hearer as true ('wisdom')[11]

A proverb is an invention of individual, who uses ideas, words and ways of speaking (usually short, easy to remember and figurative) that are generally familiar to express a truth based upon observation and experience. Because Thompson put into concise words what others had already felt, his sayings win acceptance and circulate in tradition.

The most significant quality of a proverb is wisdom, both moral and practical, handed over from one generation to the other. Joyce Penfield comments: "Proverbs are in effect quotes from the ancestors."[12] A proverb is moral advice based on experience and observation. Westermarck observes: "The proverbial statements are expressive of all sorts of observations, opinions, and feelings, but an instructive tendency is common to most of them."[13]

---

[10] Archer Taylor, "Wisdom of Many and Wit of One," in *The Wisdom of many: Essays on the proverb*, ed. Wolfgang Mieder & Alan Dundes (New York: Garland, 1981), 3.

[11] John Mark Thompson, *The Form and Function of Proverbs in Ancient Israel* (The Hague: Mouton and Co. N.V., 1974), 18.

[12] Joyce Penfield and Mary Duru, "Proverbs: Metaphors That Teach," *Anthropological Quarterly* 61, no. 3 (1988): 119.

[13] Edward Westermarck, *Wit and Wisdom in Morocco: A Study of Native Proverbs* (New York: Horace Liveright Inc, 1931), 2.

Proverbs are very often, either implicitly or explicitly, value-judgments.[14] This can be expressed in proverbs that say that one thing is better than another (*Your friend who is near is better than your brother who is far away*) or in proverbs that speak of the consequences of certain events (*Patience is the key of all well-being*). Many proverbs consist of advice or a command (*If you have much give from your wealth, and if you have little give from your heart*). One of the main aims of proverbs is to influence people's behavior, which often serve as guides to acceptable behavior.

The Importance of Proverbs in Arab Culture

A love of verbal expression has long been characteristic of Arab culture. In the Arabian peninsula, even in the pre-Islamic era oral poetry flourished among Arabs. Barakat notes: "Of the several genres of oral literature common in the Arab world, none is more pervasive than the proverb."[15]

Societies bound by a rigid tradition of fixed moral and religious notions and comprising a large percentage of illiterate persons usually possess a great treasure of proverbs and popular sayings, particularly if they are endowed with a rich and expressive language. The Arabic-speaking countries represent a most conspicuous example of such a society. [16]

Both classical Arabic and the Arabic dialects (e.g. Moroccan Arabic) are rich in proverbial lore. Dickson observed: "The Arab is forever quoting proverbs or sayings of some poet or other, and he seems to enjoy this almost as much as story telling."[17] Abelkafi states: "One might claim that the Arabs make more use of proverbs than most other nations."[18]

Proverbs play an important role among the Berbers in Morocco. The main reason for this is that *Tamazight* (a collective name of Berber languages) has a strong oral character and proverbs are particularly popular in oral societies.

---

[14] Wolfgang Mieder lists 55 definitions of proverbs on Wolfgang Mieder, "Popular Views Of The Proverb," *Deproverbio.com*, 1999, http://www.deproverbio.com/DPjournal/DP,5,2,99/MIEDER/VIEWS.htm. (accessed February 20, 2006).

[15] R.A. Barakat, *A Contextual Study of Arabic Proverbs*, FF Communications, vol. XCVI, no. 226 (Helsinki: Suomalainen Tiedeakatemia, 1980), 5.

[16] S.D. Goitein, "The Present-Day Arabic Proverbs as a Testimony to the Social History of the Middle East," in *S.D. Goitein Studies in Islamic History and Institutions*, (Leiden: E.J. Brill, 1966), 361.

[17] Sheila K. Webster, "Arabic Proverbs and Related Forms," in *Proverbium: Yearbook of International Proverb Scholarship* (Burlington, Vermont: University of Vermont, 1986), 180.

[18] Ibid.

Abdes El Ajjouri, a Moroccan living in Belgium, who has written a thesis on Tamazight proverbs, says: "The proverbs seem to be used to oil the wheels of the social machine along with other traditional oral and kinetic expressions."[19]

R.A. Barakat lists the following factors inherent in Arab society and culture, as reasons for the wide use and dissemination of Arabic proverbs[20]:

1. The vast pride Arabs take in being able to invoke such sayings when the need arises.
2. The respect afforded any person who is capable of using these sayings correctly.
3. The emotional attachment Arabs have for their colloquial and written language.
4. The emphasis Arabs place on learning (wisdom) i.e., not necessarily derived from institutionalized knowledge.
5. The reverence Arabs have for their past and tradition.
6. The great stress Moslems place on the Holy Book as a body of religious and spiritual teachings, as a source of law, and as a code of behavior.
7. The respect Moslems have for the *Hadith* of the Prophet Muhammad and the *sunna* associated with him.

He suggests that reverence which Arabs have for their history and traditions, as well as their respect for wisdom explains why proverbs are so frequently applied to specific contexts, "For the proverb is the linguistic embodiment of traditional wisdom."

Arabic proverbs bear the stamp of approval from tradition and are thought to best express one's thoughts on many occasions."[21] In the Arab world someone's statements have more credibility if he uses proverbs, because "from the point of view of the listeners, he documents his conversation by giving it authority of past usage."[22]

Barakat even states that any person not using proverbs and other sayings in his conversations is suspect, because "by using proverbs, he shifts the responsibility of his content to past traditions and authorities whose wisdom cannot be questioned. To be a successful conversationalist in the Arab world, such 'documentation' is required by one's audience."[23]

---

[19] From a personal letter from Abdes El Ajjouri to the author on February 22, 2005.
[20] R.A. Barakat, *A Contexual Study of Arabic Proverbs*. FF Communications, vol. XCVI, no. 226. (Helsinki: Suomalainen Tiedeakatemia, 1980), 7, 8.
[21] Ibid., 10.
[22] Ibid., 11.
[23] Ibid., 12.

In Morocco, this veneration of the past, which is important in society, explains the high value attached to proverbs:

> In the typical oral Moroccan culture, proverbs serve as a strong moralizing device. Their 'rhyming' structure makes them easy to remember, their construction on a paradox appeals to the ear, their ideologically-laden messages cannot be easily contested by their users, and the 'taken-for-granted' truths they express are believed to embody the wisdom of previous generations and are, hence, considered a valuable legacy and a permanent source of advice, in a society that venerates the past. Like citations, proverbs are not easily contested because they are presented in a way which excludes any personal commitment or possibility of issuing a value judgment on the part of interlocutors. [24]

Sources of Arabic Proverbs

Knowing that proverbs play a significant role in Arab and Moroccan society, it is of interest to find out what the sources are for these proverbs, as this would help us to understand whether we can expect similarities between Moroccan proverbs and the book of Proverbs. Also, the fact that a vast number of proverbs are common to most of the Arab countries stimulates an interest to investigate their origins "particularly if one bears in mind that this common stock is characteristically different from the proverbs of other areas, including the European."[25]

The sources for the Arabic and Moroccan proverbs that have been identified are discussed below:

The Qur'an and the Hadith

The Moroccan society is deeply influenced by their religion, which is Islam. "This becomes obvious if one pays attention to the linguistic production of Moroccans in their everyday life. The Koran, God and the prophet are continually referred to. The Moroccan radio and television start and end with the daily recitations of some verses from the Koran."[26]

---

[24] Fatima Sadiqi, *Women, Gender and Language in Morocco* (Leiden; Boston: Brill, 2003), 144.

[25] Ibid., 367.

[26] Khalid Mesbahi Idrissi, *A sociolinguistic approach to the use of proverbs in Moroccan Arabic* (Fes, Morocco: by the author, 1983), 7.

The Moroccan proverbs are in many respects reflections of their Islamic culture. In Moroccan proverbs:

> God is often mentioned, and always in a reverent manner. The religious duties of almsgiving and prayer are strongly emphasized, and the same is the case with patience and resignation, so frequently enjoined in the Koran, and propriety of behavior, on which the Islamic traditions have so much to say. Other Muhammadan characteristics are the deference shown to refugees and guests, the low opinion held about women, the belief in curses and the evil eye.[27]

Folk Stories and Fables

Folk stories and fables are a means of entertainment among people in Morocco, especially among the old: "It is very common to find grandmothers or grandfathers narrating these stories to their grandsons and granddaughters before the latter go to bed. These stories are usually intended to teach moral lessons. Consequently, one or two sentences, usually the last in the story, are quoted to be used as proverbs."[28]

A Specific Wise Man

Many Moroccan proverbs have their origin in a specific wise man. "This wise man in the Moroccan culture is Sidi Abderrahmane Lmajdoub, who lived in the 16th century. He was a mystic, who expressed his truth by means of poetry. Moroccans who have found in him a source of wisdom refer use part of his poetry as proverbs."[29]

Jokes and Songs

Although the phenomena of jokes and songs are universal to all languages and cultures, "Moroccans in this field have gone further than other nations by extracting proverbs from their famous jokes and popular songs."[30]

Arab World

Many Moroccan proverbs originated from other parts of the Arab world. Goitein states that approximately one-third of the modern Arabic proverbs recorded thus far are common to the greater part of the Arab world. [31]

---

[27] Westermarck, 51.
[28] Idrissi, 8, 9.
[29] Ibid., 10.
[30] Ibid., 12.
[31] Goitein, 365.

Pre-Arabic near Eastern Aramaic Proverbs

Goitein, who has traced many Arabic proverbs through the centuries, believes that the pre-Islamic Arab proverb has totally disappeared, while pre-Arabic Near Eastern proverbs have survived in Arabic speech:

> The eclipse of the ancient Arabic proverb is paralleled by the survival of the pre-Arabic Near Eastern proverb in Arabic speech. The countries of the Fertile Crescent, i.e. Iraq, Northern Mesopotamia, Syria, Lebanon and Palestine, possessed a common language before the Arab conquest: Aramaic. Many of the most current and most characteristic of vernacular Arabic proverbs are but translations or adaptations from the Aramaic. [32]

> The percentage of Aramaic proverbs contained in the vernaculars of North Africa, Egypt, North Arabia or Yemen is not considerably smaller than the proportion of those found in the countries of the Fertile Crescent, which had been Aramaic-speaking before Islam. It appears that the Aramaic proverb had partly found its way into Arabic speech even before the advent of Islam.[33]

Jewish Proverbs

There has been a long co-existence between the Arabs and the Jews throughout the history. "We become aware of it when we pay attention to the linguistic production of either group, since each has affected the other."[34] "Conformity of the Arabic with the Jewish proverb is simply due to the fact that the Jewish literature represents a treasure house of the popular speech prevalent in the Near East prior to the rise of Islam."[35]

Western Languages

In Morocco, many proverbs seem to have been borrowed from English or French. Idrissi observes that "people, unconsciously use the translated form of these proverbs, that they acquired during the process of learning the native language of the proverb."[36] This means that those who are illiterate or educated only in Arabic or Berber might not know these proverbs.

---

[32] Ibid., 371.
[33] Ibid., 376.
[34] Idrissi, 14.
[35] Goitein, 373.
[36] Idrissi, 13.

Other Sources

Although many proverbs might have originated thousands or hundreds of years ago, as language is alive, new proverbs are still created. The Moroccan proverb *the year of wealth and the young king,* which is used by people when they feel joyful, originated in 1927 when King Mohammed V was crowned, and in which year there was a good harvest. [37]

No Known Origin

Of course there remain many proverbs in Morocco of which the source is not known. Some may be locally created by the natives, others have may have originated from other parts of the world. The fact that some of the present Moroccan proverbs even originated from the Bible is an option that is left open by a Moroccan researcher:

> English and French have some borrowed Latin and Biblical proverbs in their respective proverbial repertoires; therefore can we say that Moroccan Arabic has borrowed some Latin and Biblical proverbs through English and French? The answer to such questions will probably remain a mystery, but it is interesting to speculate.[38]

The fact that this is mentioned as a possibility by a Moroccan Muslim is an encouragement for Christians to explore this further. Could it be that like the Apostle Paul in Athens used the altar to the unknown God as a bridge to preach the Gospel, we can use the proverbs of 'unknown source' as a bridge to share the Good News with Muslims? This question will be discussed later.

Functions of Proverbs in Moroccan Society

Having seen the important role that proverbs play in Moroccan society and having looked at some of its sources, it is worthwhile now to turn our attention to the functions that proverbs perform. It is clear that proverbs are not only reflections of life, but they also play an active part in it.[39] What is it they are used for and when? Westermarck, who lived in Morocco in the early part of the 20th century, and who has studied Moroccan proverbs extensively, writes:

> When a person has something to say, a proverb often gives him a convenient ready-made means of expression which spares him the trouble of finding words of his own for formulating his thought. The use of a proverb

---

[37] Ibid., 14.
[38] Ibid., 15.
[39] Westermarck, 54.

adds piquancy to one's speech; it shows savoir vivre and knowledge too; it makes a neat argument which has the authority of custom and tradition.[40]

Khalid Idrissi, who researched proverbs in Moroccan Arabic in the 1980s, writes:

> Proverbs are used everywhere and any time. People tend to use them to give more emphasis to their statements, to make them sound more beautiful, in order to appear impressive, and to show their ability in manipulating language skillfully. People find them useful because they help speakers convey what they want to say. A proverb can sometimes be used as a summary of a speech. The proverb might also be used by the addressee when he understands what the speaker is talking about. His proverb comes as a conclusion to the idea talked about.[41]

Abdes El-Ajjouri, who studied the function of Proverbs among Berbers in Morocco in more recent times, comes to a similar conclusion:

> By using the proverb the old and wise Amazigh takes a careful and diplomatic stand, without offending the person he is speaking with. He passes on wisdom, based on experience and orally handed down from generation to generation, to counsel his children, to expose the selfishness, injustice, hypocrisy, covetousness of his countrymen. Through a proverb he can come to the point, without too much indirectness.[42]

In Moroccan culture someone's honor and dignity are one of the most cherished possessions, putting someone to shame in front of others is one of the worst things you can do. Being indirect is therefore considered a high value and very polite. This explains many of the functions proverbs have in Moroccan society, several of which are listed below.

To Warn and Advise

Proverbs in Moroccan society are sometimes used to warn and give advise: "These strategies, that are most used by the old to the young, are a means of teaching the young or making them aware of elders' experience. The proverbs that fulfill these functions are conclusions or summaries of the past experiences of previous generations."[43]

---

[40] Westermarck, 55.
[41] Idrissi, 20.
[42] In a personal letter to the author on February 22, 2005.
[43] Idrissi, 16.

To Express Dissatisfaction or Disapproval

One of the feelings that figure prominently in Moroccan proverbs is dissatisfaction. Complaints frequently take the form of proverbs.[44]

To Defend One's Behavior

Proverbs are not only a suitable vehicle to criticize someone or something, but also to defend one's behavior, when being reproved or laughed at.

To Give Hope and Consolation

Besides proverbs that express dissatisfaction, others are specifically used to give hope and consolation.

For Humoristic Purposes

Proverbs in Morocco are also used for humoristic purposes. This kind of proverb is mainly used among young people. "Many jokes in Moroccan Arabic are known as 'dirty jokes' that is jokes that are about sex or that contain taboo words. This strategy has its equivalent in proverbs too. Some of them provoke laughter when heard."[45]

To Convey Irony

Ironical proverbs are another characteristic of Moroccan society. Moroccans when talking about each other tend to use these proverbs as a comment. This it makes the sarcasm less offensive, by making it less personal. "When they notice a flaw in somebody, their tongue quickly finds the exact description that suits the person."[46]

To Curse

Some proverbs in Morocco are being used to curse. "What is peculiar about them is that they are only joking curses. When the speaker utters them, he does not really intend to see the addressee suffering from what he has asked to befall him. Such proverbs suggest intimacy rather than hatred, between speaker and addressee."[47]

---

[44]   Westermarck, 55.
[45]   Idrissi, 18.
[46]   Ibid., 19.
[47]   Ibid., 19.

To Bring Goodwill and Peace

While proverbs can be used to curse someone, Westermarck notes that proverbs can also serve to bring goodwill and peace. "The use of an appropriate proverb may serve to cool the rage, stop the quarrel, and make those who were cursing each other a moment before rejoice and shake hands with each other."[48]

Situational Use of Proverbs

Predominantly, proverbs are used in conversations among people, and as Idrissi notes: "There are no restrictions, either on the settings where they are used, or the times of their use."[49] Besides in personal conversations, proverbs in Morocco are also being used in other ways:

Advertisements

Proverbs are used in advertising on Moroccan television to increase the influence of the advertisement on the audience. Wolfgang Mieder, who has studied the use of proverbs in advertising, says: "Proverbs are used because their familiar sound creates a feeling of positive identification and trustworthy authority."[50]

Political Speech

In one of his speeches late King Hassan II, when talking about the commitment of Moroccans to their Sahara, summarized all he said in a single proverb.[51]

Class

Lecturers and teachers tend to use proverbs in class, either to make the idea explained more explicit to the student, or teach him a language through proverbs.[52]

Songs and Drama

In one play that was shown on Moroccan television, within one hour nine proverbs were used. "The playwright, who relied on symbolism, used a set of

---

[48] Westermarck, 63.

[49] Idrissi, 20.

[50] Wolfgang Mieder, "Tradition and Innovation: Proverbs in Advertising," *Journal of Popular Culture*, no. 11 (1977): 310.

[51] Idrissi, 21.

[52] Ibid., 22.

proverbs, to make his play clearer to ordinary people, who are not educated enough to understand symbolism."[53]

Public Discussion

During public meetings Moroccans regularly use proverbs to strengthen their arguments in a discussion.[54]

In Electronic Signature

Sometimes Moroccan use proverbs as part of their electronic signature, when sending out e-mail messages.[55]

Future of Proverbs in Arab Society

We've seen that proverbs play an important role in Arab and Moroccan society (both among Arabs and Berbers). But as proverbs have originated as an oral folklore genre, the question can be asked whether they still have a function in our literate culture.

In light of Idrissi's comment that "proverbs are much more related to ordinary people, or the lower classes than they are to upper class people,"[56] the question whether with the increased literacy and education, the use of proverbs might disappear, is legitimate.

Despite the fact that the younger generation seem to make less use of proverbs,[57] it remains to be seen whether we'll witness the disappearance of the use of proverbs, as a result of increased literacy and education. Not only because Arabic proverbs are used as a device in modern literature, and the estimated the national literacy rate in Morocco is about 60% of the adult population,[58] but mainly because the use of proverbs fits very neatly into some important aspects of Arab and Moroccan culture:

---

[53] Ibid., 23.
[54] http://www.nieuwenederlandsespreekwoorden.nl/spreekwoorden/pages/spreek woorden.html.
[55] Observed personally by the author in e-mail messages received from Moroccan friends.
[56] Idrissi, 23.
[57] Although, looking at the Moroccan websites, (e.g. http://www.MaghrebOnline. nl and http://www.Tawiza.nl), that are mainly geared towards the younger generation, the use of Moroccan proverbs and its meaning regularly come up.
[58] *Unicef,* "At A Glance: Morocco," http://www.unicef.org/infobycountry/moro cco_statistics.html. (accessed February 25,2006).

Arabs have always had a particular taste for brief, concise and witty idioms and proverbs. It is doubtful whether increased literacy and education have seriously affected the quality and quantity of proverbial speech, at least in Arabic culture. Arabs' gatherings, formal and informal, are marked by highly formalized relationships. A formalized relationship gives rise to highly predictable and normalized language such as idioms and proverbs. [59]

Also, honor and shame play an important role in Moroccan culture and proverbs are an ideal way to save face and to be polite and indirect in bringing your point across in disagreements and arguments.

Another reason for the expectation that proverbs will not easily disappear from the Moroccan culture is that Arabs put more value on experience than on science. "The proverb *Ask a man of experience not a doctor* provides evidence of the psychology of the Arabs who believe more in their experiences than in science. This is still a persistent phenomenon in Moroccan society."[60]

Conclusion

Throughout the centuries proverbs have played a significant role in Arab society. This is also true of Morocco, both among the Arabs and the Berbers.

As a means to justify one's one behavior and influence someone else's, it is employed by different people for several different purposes. Although the main usage is in personal conversations, proverbs are also used in other media.

Proverbs clearly have their origin in oral, illiterate cultures, but there seems to be no reason to presume that its usage will disappear in the modern times of increased education and literacy. This is particularly so in Morocco, not only because about half of the Morocco adult population is still illiterate, but also as has been pointed out proverbs as a means of communication fits well in a society that gives great weight to honor and shame. In such a context proverbs are an excellent way to communicate in an indirect way.

The fact that proverbs are still being used in Moroccan society to communicate familiar truth, should encourage us in our exploration whether the book of Proverbs can be used as a tool to communicate the unfamiliar truth of the Gospel with our Moroccan friends.

---

[59] Mahmoud Aziz F. Yassin, "Spoken Arabic Proverbs," *Bulletin of the School of Oriental and African Studies*, no. 51 (1988): 59-68.

[60] Idrissi, 13.

Chapter 2

Making Sense of the Book of Proverbs

Because the book of Proverbs occupies a central place in this study, it is important that we have a good understanding of the structure, content and theology of this book of the Bible. It is beyond the scope of this book to discuss all the discussion that is taking place among scholars regarding the authorship, theology and relationship with non-Biblical sources, therefore this chapter will highlight those matters that have a direct bearing upon the goal of this study.

Origins and Background

Authorship

Although it seems that the authorship of Proverbs is established in the first verse: "These are the proverbs of Solomon, David's son, king of Israel" (Prov. 1:1), the issue is not that simple. Whybray says: "The traditional view which attributed the whole book to Solomon has long since been given up in critical scholarship."[61] It is fair to add that this is also true for most of the conservative, evangelical scholarship.

That Solomon did not author the whole book seems obvious from the fact that other authors are mentioned in the book. The book contains notices of authorship at 1:1, 10:1, 22:17, 24:23, 25:1, 30:1, and 31:1. The book of Proverbs is clearly an anthology: a collection of collections. Waltke divides the book into seven sections.[62] From this, one could draw the following list:

Table 1. Overview divisions and authorship Book of Proverbs

Section	Chapter	Authorship
I	1-9	Solomon
II	10:1-22:16	Solomon

---

[61] R.N. Whybray, *The Book of Proverbs: A Survey of Modern Study* (Leiden: Brill, 1995), 150.

[62] Bruce K. Waltke, *The Book of Proverbs, Chapters 1-15* (Grand Rapids, Michigan: William B. Eerdmans Publishing Company, 2004), 9-28.

Section	Chapter	Authorship
III	22:17-24:22	wise men
IV	24:23-34	wise men
V	25-29	Solomon (as copied by Hezekiah's men)
VI	30	Agur, son of Jakeh
VII	31:1-31	Lemuel

But, despite the notice of authorship in 1:1, many scholars reject Solomonic authorship for section I. They believe that the words in 1:1 are a general heading for the entire book and not an indication of the authorship of chapters 1-9.[63] On the other hand Steinmann concludes:

> On every level examined – vocabulary, thought, and mode of expression – Proverbs 1-9 indicates that it comes from the same author as 10:1-22:16 and 25-29, exactly as the book itself indicates. While the "fear of the Lord" motif is obvious to readers, it would require an extremely sensitive reading of 10:1-22:16 (and 25-29) by a different writer to produce such a closely aligned text as 1-9. The probabilities of 1-9 coming from someone other than Solomon, therefore, are extremely low. Moreover, the vocabulary usage shared by 1-9, 10:1-22:16 and 25-29 argues for a common author, because it would have been unthinkably difficult for a different author to have produced such a similar pattern of word usage.[64]

This book is based on the conviction that Solomon is the author of chapters 1-22, and that chapters 25-29 contain his proverbs, collected by the men of Hezekiah. From 1 Kings 4:32 we know that Solomon spoke 3,000 proverbs, therefore Solomon's proverbs found in the book of Proverbs are only a fraction of his total repertoire. Steinmann states that:

> The inclusion (but not authorship) of the Words of the Wise (22:17-24:22 and 24:23-34) most probably should also be attributed to Solomon. These are somewhat like his writings, and may have influenced him to some extent. On the other hand, he may have recognized in them thoughts similar to his own, and included them for that reason.[65]

---

[63] E.g. Derek Kidner and Alan P. Ross, cited by Andrew E. Steinmann, "Proverbs 1-9 As A Solomonic Composition," *Journal of the Evangelical Theological Society* 43.4 (December 2000): 659, 660.

[64] Steinmann, 674.

[65] Ibid.

Nothing much is known about the other authors named in the book, although because of our purpose, two authors, Agur and Lemuel, deserve special attention.

Arab Authors in Proverbs?

Two of the unknown authors in Proverbs are Agur (30:1) and Lemuel (31:1). There is a lot of confusion among scholars as to the meaning of the word *massa* in both verses. The main question is whether this term is to be understood as a reference to a prophetic oracle, or as a proper name. This is not the place to discuss the pro's and con's of each position. According to John Day, the majority of scholars today translate *massa* as a proper name instead of "an oracle,"[66] and this is taken as the presupposition in this book. That way Proverb 30:1 would read: "The sayings of Agur, son of Yakeh, king of Massa" and Proverbs 31:1 would read: "The sayings of King Lemuel, king of Massa". Massa is mentioned as one of the descendants of Ishmael in Genesis 25:14. Therefore it is likely that *massa* refers to an Ishmaelite kingdom. The names Agur, Yakeh and Lemuel are not attested in Old Testament literature. But Agur and Yakeh have been attested in the body of names of south and north Arabia. And Lemuel also occurs in south Arabian inscriptions as a woman's proper name.[67] "Thus Agur and Lemuel were Arab sages from 'the descendants of Hagar who seek wisdom on the earth (Baruch 3:23).' They must have found the truth in God's revelation through their Hebrew kin."[68] Delitzsch concludes his discussion on the identity of these biblical figures by saying: "We regard it as more probable that King Lemuel and his countryman Agur were Ishmaelites who had raised themselves above the religion of Abraham (Din Ibrahim, a belief, which along with Mosaism, continues among nomadic tribes in north Arabia) and recognized the religion of Israel as its completion."[69] Maalouf concludes: "By displaying strong piety and a knowledge of Yahweh (Proverbs 30:2-9; 31:1, 8) these two sages are clear examples of conversions to Yahweh among the Gentiles, particularly Israel's closest kin, the Arabian descendants of Abraham through Ishmael."[70]

Date

As any anthology, Proverbs is composed of material written over a period of time. We do not know how long, because there are anonymous sections of

---

[66] Tony Maalouf, *Arabs in the Shadow of Israel* (Grand Rapids: Kregel Publications, 2003), 138.

[67] Ibid., 141.

[68] Ibid., 142.

[69] Ibid., 143.

[70] Ibid., 143.

the book as well as named authors about whom we know nothing. Solomon lived in the tenth century B.C. Chapter 25:1 shows that the book was still in the making in the time of Hezekiah (ca. 700 B.C.), about 250 years after Solomon. It is assumed that chapters 30 and 31 were added later as existing collections. It is reasonable to infer that there was an even later editorial stage that arranged the entire book and provided the short introduction (1:1-7). The exact date of this final editing is not known.

Meaning of the Term 'Proverb'

The term 'proverb' is difficult to define. The Hebrew word *masal*, the plural form of which identifies the book of Proverbs, points to two possible meanings: 'a similitude' or 'a powerful word'. The first sense of *masal* derives from the verb which means 'to be like', the second, from the meaning 'to rule'. The former emphasizes the analogy that lies at the heart of every proverb, while the latter stresses its paradigmatic or exemplary character. Therefore "'saying' best retains the openness of the Hebrew word *masal*."[71]

Structure

The material in chapters 1-9, which consists of relatively long poems, is quite different from the short proverbs of the sentence literature in the chapters that follow.

Most scholars believe that chapters 1-9 function as a deliberate introduction, thus inviting the reader to exercise imagination in interpreting the sayings that follow. Proverbs 1-9 help us to make sense of the hundreds of individual sayings in the rest of the book. "The introductory chapters (1-9) provide the hermeneutical grid through which the rest of the book should be read, thus placing a profound theological nuance on the individual proverbs in the rest of the book."[72]

Proverbs 1-9 teaches that there are two paths: one that is right and leads to life, and one that is wrong and leads to death. The son is walking the path of life, and the father and Wisdom are warning him of the dangers he will encounter as well as the encouragement he will find. The most important people encountered along the way, and this explains why we need to understand that the addressee is a man, are two women: Woman Wisdom and the dark figure of Woman Folly. This will be dealt with in more detail in chapter five.

---

[71] James L. Crenshaw, *Old Testament Wisdom; An Introduction* (London: SCM Press Ltd, 1982), 67.

[72] Raymond B. Dillard and Tremper Longman III, *An Introduction to the OT* (Grand Rapids Michigan: Zondervan Publishing House, 1994), 242.

In the rest of the book we find the sayings we recognize as proverbs: short, self-contained, poured out apparently at random. Although some scholars have tried to find units of assembled verses, Kidner writes: "Once is a while there will be a small cluster round a single theme, but the standard unit is a single verse."[73]

The Context of the Book of Proverbs

Relationship to the Surrounding Ancient World

In light of our purpose, it is important to address the context of the book of Proverbs, particularly with regard to the surrounding ancient world. "By wisdom the Lord laid the earth's foundations, by understanding he set the heavens in place" (Proverbs 3:19),[74] implies that because God has created the world and has left His mark on it, we can see His glory reflected in many aspects. In the book of Proverbs we become aware of our fellow men as human beings rather than as Israelites or Gentiles. The book emphasizes that: "God is broader than worship, ethics, evangelism and eschatology, and has a voice in sociology, education, art and science."[75]

During Solomon's reign there was a lot of interaction going on with the rest of the world. Not only did he have a fleet of trading ships who returned once every three years carrying goods from abroad (1 Kings 10:22), but "people from all nations came to listen to Solomon's wisdom, sent by all the kings of the world" (1 Kings 4:34).

> To engage with mind-sharpening encounters with all corners of the world (as Solomon did) was to bring one's beliefs out into the open. It implied that the truth one lived by was valid through and through, and that its writ ran everywhere; it also suggested that shared ground existed between the truly wise of any nation. In 1 Kings 4:30, 31 Solomon's wisdom is compared with that of the East and of Egypt, as well as that of his fellow Israelites. True, he outshone them all; but there was a basis of comparison between them. It was because his wisdom surpassed rather than by-passed theirs, that they flocked to hear him.[76]

---

[73] Derek Kidner, *The Wisdom of Proverbs, Job & Ecclesiastes; An introduction to Wisdom Literature* (Leicester: Inter-Varsity Press, 1985), 25.

[74] The translation of the Bible used in this chapter and throughout this book that of New International Version, unless mentioned otherwise.

[75] Ibid., 14.

[76] Ibid., 15.

1 Kings 4:29-31 does not disparage the wisdom of other nations; it simply says that Solomon's wisdom surpassed theirs. "In and of itself, this encourages our examination of biblical wisdom in the light of wisdom traditions of the surrounding nations."[77]

The Bible itself alludes to the wisdom of Egypt and Mesopotamia (1 Kings 4: 30; Daniel 1:4, 17, 20). The genre of wisdom literature was common in the ancient world and the more we learn from this the more we discover the affinities that the book of Proverbs has with literature from other countries.

General knowledge of wisdom sayings across the ancient Near East as well as specific interchange between Egypt and Solomon's court make a literary connection between *the Instruction of Amenope* (1580-1100 BC) and the book of Proverbs likely. Although no scholar seems to deny that there is a relationship between *Amenope* and a substantial section of Proverbs 22:17-24:22, the nature of the relationship between the two texts has been disputed. The two main options are: (a) the author of Proverbs 22:17ff knew *Amenope* and adapted it to suit his own purpose; (b) the author of *Amenope* knew Proverbs 22:17ff. and adapted it similarly.[78]

Believing that "Inspiration does not exclude the divine use of existing material; but in Scripture it takes on a new force, a higher meaning, and becomes authoritative,"[79] we can accept that *Amenope* is generally seen as forming the background of Proverbs 22:17-24:22.

According to various scholars there are some similarities between the book of Proverbs and the *Instruction of Ani* (c 1100 BC), particularly in the warnings against adultery. Also the *Instruction of Oncheheshony* (c 400-300 BC) includes instructions that are similar to Proverbs 27:10 and 17:21. Mesopotamia also had collections of proverbial material. The *Words of Ahiqar* (700-670 B.C.) is a collection of proverbs, riddles, short fables, and religious observations. Some of the content reflects the truth expressed in Proverbs 13:24 and 27:3).[80]

But even though the collections share some of the same interests, the biblical material is unique in its prerequisite of a personal faith in a personal God. To the Hebrews the success of wisdom did not simply require a compliance

---

[77] Tremper Longman III, *How to Read Proverbs* (Leicester: InterVarsity Press, 2002), 62.

[78] Whybray discusses the relationship between Proverbs and Amenope in detail in his book 'The Book of Proverbs: A Survey of Modern Study', 6-14.

[79] Allan P. Ross, *The Expositor's Bible Commentary*, ed. Frank E. Gaebelein, *Volume 5* (Grand Rapids, Michigan: The Zondervan Corporation, 1991), 884.

[80] Ibid., 885.

with wise instructions but trust in, reverence for, and submissions to the Lord (Proverbs 1:7;3:5-6;9:10), who created everything and governs both the world of nature and human history (3:19-20; 16:4; 21:1).

Any ancient wisdom used by the Hebrews had to harmonize with this religious world view, and any ancient wisdom used in this collection took on greater significance when subordinated to the true faith.[81]

To recognize biblical texts as divine revelation does not necessarily mean that all their contents had to be previously unknown information. On the contrary, before many of these facts and concepts were written down, they were passed on verbally from generation to generation and consequently could have circulated over vast distances and found their way into many diverse cultures. Therefore, whatever the Spirit of God inspired the ancient writers to include became a part of the Word of the Lord. Such inclusions then took on a new and greater meaning when they formed part of Scripture; in a word, they became authoritative and binding, part of the communication of the divine will. Ross states:

> Very likely the writers deliberately used well-known concepts and expressions from the pagan world to subordinate them to the true religion. For example, while Maat was a deity of justice and order in Egypt, no such deity existed in Israel. Rather, hokmah ("wisdom") was personified and spoke its message in the first person – something maat did not do. By incorporating wise sayings and motifs (in addition to producing new and unparalleled sayings) and investing them with the higher religious value, the Hebrew sages were in a sense putting new wine into old wine skins. They could forcefully teach, then, that true wisdom was from above and not from below.[82]

Relation to the Old Testament

Although the book of Proverbs is the focus of this book, it is important to always keep in mind that the book is not an island. It is part of the Scriptures and not in contradiction with it.

It is beyond the scope of this book to bring out the relationships between the book of Proverbs and the rest of the Old Testament, in which wisdom plays an important role. Although Solomon is called the wisest man on earth, there are other wise men in the history of Israel and wisdom sayings are found in other parts of the Old Testament. In fact, there was a saying, quoted in Jeremiah 18:18 that: "The law shall not perish from the priest, nor counsel

---

[81]   Ibid.

[82]   Ibid., 886.

from the wise, nor the word from the prophet". This verse seems to underline that wisdom was one of the three main channels of revelation.

Murphy has drawn attention to the similarities between the book of Deuteronomy and the book of Proverbs.[83] Tremper Longman III cautions to keep the book of Proverbs in close harmony with the other two so-called Wisdom books in the Old Testament: Job and Ecclesiastes.[84]

Relation to the New Testament

Because chapter four will discuss the relationship between Proverbs and the New Testament in greater detail, all that will be said here is that about twenty quotations or allusions from Proverbs appear in the New Testament. Jesus used the teaching of Proverbs several times as a basis for his parables.[85]

Are Proverbs always True?

The more we see the Bible as an organic unit, the less we run the risk to absolute the proverbs. To read a proverb as if it were always true in every circumstance is to commit a serious error. Tremper Longman III rightly says: "The proverb form, no matter the cultural background, presupposes the right circumstance for its proper application. Proverbs are not universally valid. Their validity depends on the right time and the right circumstance."[86]

Purpose

The book of Proverbs leaves us in no doubt as to its purpose, which is clearly stated in the opening verses of the book:

These are the wise sayings of Solomon, David's son, Israel's king – Written down so we'll know how to live well and right, to understand what life means and where it's going. A manual for living, for learning what's right and just and fair; To teach the inexperienced the ropes and give our young people a grasp on reality. There's something here also for seasoned men and women,

---

[83] Roland E. Murphy, "Can the Book of Proverbs be a Player in "Biblical Theology"?," *Biblical Theology Bulletin*, no. 31 (2001), 5.

[84] Tremper Longman III, 89.

[85] The contribution of the book of Proverbs to the New Testament life and thought is cited in: Charles T. Fritsch, "The Gospel in the Book of Proverbs," *Theology Today*, April, 1950, 169-183.

[86] Tremper Longman III, 48, 49.

still a thing or two for the experienced to learn – Fresh wisdom to probe and penetrate, the rhymes and reasons of wise men and women.[87]

Is Proverbs a Secular Book?

Although more than 100 verses, which is more than 10% of the total number of verses in the book of Proverbs, contain direct references to God,[88] the book is sometimes considered to be a secular book. It is true that this collection of wise sayings is not exclusively religious: its teachings apply to human problems in general and not primarily to the problems of the religious community or to major theological themes such as election, redemption, and covenant. Rather, the teacher of wisdom concerns himself with people as plain, ordinary individuals who live in the world, and with the wisdom and folly of their attitudes and actions in the common things of life.

It is an astonishing fact, repeatedly pointed out by scholars, that there are no references in Proverbs to historical accounts and traditions like those of the patriarchal narratives, the Exodus, Sinai, the law or the covenant. The bulk of the proverbs in the book of Proverbs don't seem to have any specific reference to the religious life in Israel.

The number of references in the book to acts of worship – sacrifice, the making of vows and prayer – is very small. Whybray believes that the few references to sacrifice and prayer in chapter 10-29 "are mainly concerned with making the point that worship is acceptable to God only if offered by the righteous."[89] He believes that "this lack of references to history in the wisdom literature seems to be intentional and is probably, like the generality in its theological references, due to the specific intentions of wisdom writers to express truths and deal with problems that are timeless and common to all peoples."[90]

This could make Proverbs an evangelistic tool *par excellence*. The sayings in Proverbs focus wholly on individuals and on their concerns without restriction to specific national affiliations. They are applicable to all people at any period in history and in this sense may be characterized as universalistic. It would be wrong, however, to conclude that Proverbs is a secular book:

---

[87] Paraphrase by Eugene Peterson, *The Message* (Colorado Springs: NavPress Publishing Group, 1996).

[88] L. Boström, *The God of the Sages: The Portrayal of God in the Book of Proverbs* (Stockholm: Almqvist & Wiksell, 1990), 35.

[89] Whybray, 133.

[90] Ibid., 33.

One's understanding of the theological thinking reflected in the book of Proverbs depends in large measure on whether the theological statements are regarded as standing in harmonious unity with the remaining ninety percent or to be isolated from the rest of the book and regarded as a corrupting element.

Indeed, throughout the Masoretic text's arrangement of the book of Proverbs, theological and non-theological statements are found side by side. [91]

It seems more appropriate to believe that Proverbs integrates theology into daily life. Boström comments: "Our view is that stark antithesis between empirical knowledge and revelation, between salvation-history and everyday experience, between wisdom traditions and others does not exist in the OT."[92]

In the final analysis, we must conclude with Plaut that in Proverbs: "There are no secular proverbs which can be contrasted with religious ones; everything on earth serves the purposes of God and is potentially holy."[93]

Theology

Although Proverbs does not put forward a systematic theology and is not a book characterized by theological reflection, but a work of a primarily theological-ethical nature, we can draw some theology from Proverbs.

Four doctrines in particular seem to be relevant for our purpose because, on one hand these bring us closer to our Muslim friends, but on the other hand reveal they significant differences: The doctrine of creation, the doctrine of Wisdom, the doctrine of God and the doctrine of Man.

The Doctrine of Creation

Estes believes that "the most fundamental assumption of the worldview represented in Proverbs 1-9 is that the universe is Yahweh's creation."[94]

The book of Proverbs invites us to study our whole environment, not simply that part of it which bears directly on the covenant or on morality. It makes us look at our fellow men as human beings rather than as Israelites or Gentiles. The emphasis on creation that we find in this book provides a good reason for

---

[91]   Boström, 37.

[92]   Ibid., 44.

[93]   Ross, 890.

[94]   Daniel J. Estes, *New Studies in Biblical Theology*, ed. D.A. Carson, *Hear, my son; teaching and learning in Proverbs 1-9* (Grand Rapids, Michigan: WmB Eerdmans Publishing Co, 1997), 22.

using it in contact with Muslims, as the notion of God as the sole Creator is something that Christians and Muslims have in common. In Proverbs:

> The man of God is taking God's creatorship as seriously as his redemption, and is giving due weight to the solidarity between 'all parts of his dominion', material and immaterial, measuring all alike by the single concept of wisdom – from the universe itself down to the behavior of a colony of ants, or of a child or a courting couple, or of a buyer and seller doing business.[95]

The notion that the Lord is the sole creator is beyond doubt. It is never questioned, but uniformly presupposed and serves as a basis for ethical behavior and as a rationale for the pursuit of wisdom.

Estes draws the following implications from this doctrine:

1. Because the entire universe has its source in the creative activity of Yahweh, there is a common ethical system that applies to all humans;
2. Human meaning is found only in relationship to the Creator;
3. There is no legitimate division between sacred and secular spheres of life.[96]

The Doctrine of Wisdom

Another central doctrine in the book of Proverbs is Wisdom. The book uses several words for wisdom that make up a rainbow of constituent colors. Archer gives a description of the three major terms that are used for 'wisdom' in Proverbs:

a) *Hokma* ('wisdom'), which he defines as "practical ability to apply theory to practice"

b) *Bina* ('understanding') which he defines as "ability to discern intellectually between truth and error".

c) *Tusiyya* ('sound wisdom, efficient wisdom', or 'abiding success') which he defines as "an authentic intuition of the spiritual or psychological".[97]

In Proverbs, wisdom means being skillful and successful in one's relationships and responsibilities. It involves observing and following the Creator's principles of order in the moral universe. This order manifests God's wisdom.

---

[95] Kidner, 14.
[96] Estes, 22.
[97] Gleason Archer, *A Survey of OT Introduction* (Chicago: Moody Press, 1994), 517.

To the extent man follows this order, he is wise. In Proverbs wisdom is more than intellectual. It encompasses the moral and the religious. Although wisdom is for anyone who wants it, it is costly. It comes both by revelation (2:6) as by discipleship (2:1-5).

Kidner points out that the demands that wisdom makes are: "(1) conversion: a turning from evil (9:10; 8:13; 14:12; 9:4-6) and (2) devotion."[98] The heart of wisdom teaching is the development of responsible character.

The Doctrine of God

It is beyond the scope of this books to elaborate on the doctrine of God as found in Proverbs. Only those aspects will be mentioned that are most important for our purpose. In that respect, it is important to start with emphasizing that the book is monotheistic throughout. The concept of the Lord as the sole and sovereign creator and ruler of the universe is presupposed throughout this book. God is referred to by name in ninety-four verses in the book of Proverbs and by pronouns in eleven verses.[99] His name *Yahweh* is mentioned eighty seven times and *Elohim* seven times.[100]

A Transcendent and Sovereign God

The concept of God in the book of Proverbs is characterized by transcendence and sovereignty. The attributes of God that are mentioned mostly are His omnipotence, His omniscience, His sovereignty, His holiness and His omnipresence.

There are a number of passages (e.g. 16:1, 9; 21:30, 31; 16:33) which relate to God's sovereignty in their assertion that the Lord is able to accomplish his will independently of man's cooperation or corresponding action. The Lord is free to bring blessings or punishment upon man even if these do not correspond exactly to the person's deeds. But this does not negate His justice, which is referred to frequently (29:26; 21:12; 3:33; 10:3; 11:8; 21:12; 22:12; 12:2; 15:25; 22:22-23; 23:10,11; 20:22; 24:12; 19:17; 25:22; 3:32; 11:20; 6:17; 16:5; 6:17-19; 12:22; 11:1; 20:10,23).

A Personal God

The relationship between God and man is often described in such a way that it indicates a close personal relationship between the Lord and the individual.

---

[98] Kidner, 38.

[99] Boström, 33, 34.

[100] Bruce K. Waltke, *The Book of Proverbs, Chapters 1-15* (Grand Rapids, Michigan: William B. Eerdmans Publishing Company, 2004), 67, 68.

The book of Proverbs depicts the Lord as intimately involved in the world of man. This is made especially clear by a number of sayings expressing the Lord's concern over certain social issues. In these sayings the Lord is portrayed as a god who is closely related to individuals and desires a society characterized by justice and honesty where certain groups are not mistreated by others.[101]

The reading of Proverbs 3:12 renders the close relationship between an individual and his god in terms of the intimacy between father and son. The tenderness of this relationship is also brought into relief through the use of the word "love" – a term rarely employed in this book or elsewhere in the OT as a description of the Lord's feelings towards man. The relationship between the Lord and the upright person is thus here described in terms that points in the direction of a close, personal bond between God and man.[102]

A God who is Concerned for the Weak

The main group of people in socially difficult situations, for whom it is stated that the Lord has a special concern, are the poor (14:31; 17:5; 19:17; 22:2, 22; 29:13). Two other groups are the widow and the orphan (15:25; 23:10, 11).

A God Concerned for Social Justice

There are some sayings in Proverbs that indicate the concern of the Lord for a more general concept of social justice which is not directly related to the oppression of particular social groups (11:1; 16:11; 20:10; 20:23).

The notion that the Lord is intimately involved in the world and the life of the individual permeates Proverbs and prompts the theologically based condemnations of unjust economic practices. This explains why a very common problem of the market place (use of false weights and scales) is discussed from a religious point of view. It is remarkable that the Lord is portrayed as so intimately related to the issue. The behavior described in Proverbs 6:16-19 is not condemned so much because of its effects on other people, but because it is abhorrent to the Lord who as personal god watches over people and is concerned about justice and fair treatment of the individual.[103]

In Proverbs a view of God marked by both distance and closeness can be detected. On the one hand, God, in his role as creator and judge, is completely

---

[101] Boström, 197.
[102] Boström, 224.
[103] Ibid., 202.

beyond man. On the other hand he is concerned about the details of his creation: the harm inflicted on men is taken as though it were directed against him.

This emphasis in Proverbs on the personal nature of the sovereign Ruler of
the universe, is something that clearly distinguishes Proverbs from the Near
East wisdom literature.[104]

The Doctrine of Man

In Proverbs, the Lord is depicted as close to the person who is righteous,
fears the Lord, trusts him and is obedient to the wisdom teachings.[105]

There are a number of different expressions to designate the person who
stands in a special relationship to the Lord. The term 'righteous' is used most
frequently and it occurs around 60 times as a designation of the person who lives
an upright life and who will consequently experience success.[106] Other terms
used to designate the person close to the Lord are "upright", "those who walk in
integrity," "pious," (2:7, 8) and "those who trust in the Lord" (28:25; 29:25).

One of the virtues commended in Proverbs is diligence (10:4, 5; 12:24, 27;
14:23; 24:27) and humility (11:2; 15:33; 29:23). Other virtues mentioned: patience, self-control, reliability, generosity; truthfulness, kindness, honesty,
teachability, moderation, sobriety.

Fearing the Lord is the starting point of wisdom and also the controlling
principle or essence and heart of wisdom. The righteous way of life begins by
fearing God that is, recognizing His superiority, and responding in awe
(24:21), humility (15:33), worship (23:17, 18), love (16:6), trust (14:26), and
obedience (3:7) to God.

Moral uprightness, extolled in numerous ways in Proverbs, stems from being rightly related to God and being wise. Apart from a right relationship with
to God, moral excellence is not possible.

The terminology for the opposite character, i.e. a person from whom God
holds himself separate, is also varied. The main term used in this connection is
"wicked," often the antithesis of "righteous". Other expressions are "man of
violence" (3:31); "iniquitous person" (3:32), "scoffers" (3:34), "workers of iniq-
uity" (10:29), terms which, in the same way as the positive terminology, refer
both to the character and behavior of the person and his relationship to God.[107]

---

[104] Ibid., 208.
[105] Ibid., 213.
[106] Ibid., 213.
[107] Ibid., 215.

Vices or undesirable qualities that are mentioned in the book of Proverbs are: laziness, pride, anger, greed, envy, jealousy, drunkenness, hypocrisy, oppression, injustice, dishonesty.

With regard to life and death, the book has a lot to say, but: "the book of Proverbs never utters so much as a sigh over the prospect of natural death."[108]

"Theologically, the book has consistently implied the immortality of the righteous (2:19; 10:2, 16; 11:4, 19; 12:3, 7, 12, 19). The notion that the end of the righteous is finally death is unthinkable in this book."[109]

Conclusion

The book of Proverbs is a gathering of eight collections. Five of these collections (chapters 1-29) are words of Solomon, while two collections are attributed to Arabian converts.

The fact that there are similarities between Solomon's words and the wisdom literature from surrounding nations, underlines that Solomon, when speaking the truth about the God, used well-known concepts and expressions from the surrounding world.

There are no references to historical accounts and traditions related to the people of Israel, and hardly any references to its religious life. In the book we become aware of our fellow men as human beings rather than as Israelites or Gentiles. The sayings are applicable to all people at any period in history and in this sense may be characterized as universalistic.

Despite the similarities between Proverbs and the wisdom literature of the pagan world, and despite its universalistic nature, the book is religious true and true. It presents the world as created by a personal and transcendent God. Those who live in a right relationship with Him are truly wise and will live forever.

Its universal nature, its use of words and concepts from the pagan world, and its inclusion of Arab authors, its focus on the personal faith in a personal God are sufficient reasons to stimulate our exploration whether the book of Proverbs can be used as a bridge between its content and the wisdom of our Moroccan friends, in order to help them to acknowledge the God of Proverbs, the Father of Jesus Christ, as their Lord and Savior.

---

[108] Crenshaw, 79.

[109] William A. VanGemeren, ed., *The New International Dictionary of Old Testament Theology and Exegesis*, vol. 4, *The Topical Dictionary* (Grand Rapids: Zondervan Publishing House, 1997), 1092.

Chapter 3

Comparison between Moroccan Proverbs and the Book of Proverbs

Introduction

Having concluded in chapter one that proverbs still play a significant role in Moroccan society, it is of interest to compare some of the popular Moroccan proverbs with those mentioned in the book of Proverbs.

Three themes have been selected for a comparative study: 1) the influence of friends; 2) the use of the tongue; 3) the role of money.

These themes are well represented in Proverbs and Moroccan proverbial wisdom and are of particular interest for the goal of this study, which is to share the Good News of Jesus Christ with Moroccan immigrants, who have left family and friends behind when coming to Europe and who despite improvements are economically speaking among the poorest in their new country, while many have a hard time speaking the language of the country they and their children and grandchildren will die in.

The Influence of Friends

Contrary to the Western culture, with a strong emphasis on individualism, Moroccan culture can be considered a collectivist culture, in which family and friends play an important role and working and being with others and conforming to the group is highly emphasized. These values are also prominent in Hebrew culture, which is reflected in Proverbs, which emphasizes the importance of relationships and the need for help from others to accomplish things in life (11:14). One of the verses (15:22) is even referred to as a Moroccan proverb: *Plans fail for lack of counsel but with many advisors, succeed.*[110]

---

[110] *English Proverb Album*, "Morocco Proverbs," http://www.hometopia.com/ proverb/prov1moro.html. (accessed February 20, 2006).

Other proverbs expressing this truth are:

A single hand cannot applaud.[111]

A single bean will not make soup.[112]

A single bee will not make honey.

Kings have crowns on their heads, however they are in need of others.[113]

In Proverbs 30:27 the locusts are used as an example that even without a leader, a person can accomplish great things provided they work closely with others. A similar truth is expressed in the proverb: *Solidarity defeats even lions.*[114]

Importance of Friendship

Proverbs (17:17; 18:24) compares having 'brothers', or 'companions' with having real friends. So many brothers or companions are 'fair-weather friends', but the friend who sticks closer than a brother is the kind of friend to seek and to be. A friend loves at all times. We need 'foul-weather friends.' Any other kind of friend or friendship is not reliable. A few good friends are better than an address book full of acquaintances. A few loyal people are better than a large group of disloyal people, as is also expressed in the following proverb: *A handful of bees is better than a basketful of flies.*[115]

Friends Can Be more Valuable than Relatives

In Hebrew as well as Moroccan society, relatives are expected to care for each other, to help each other in difficult circumstances. At the same time, Proverbs states that friends bring 'joy to the heart' (29:9) and understands that in times of trouble a trustworthy neighbor, or friend, close to you both in space and in spirit, is better than a relative, who is far of both in space and in thought (27:10). A Moroccan proverb expresses the same truth in almost exactly the same words: *My close neighbor is better than my far brother.*[116] And another proverb states: *A distant fire doesn't provide warmth.*[117]

---

[111] Robert Dann, *Pretty as a Moonlit Donkey* (Chester: Jacaranda Books, 2001).

[112] Ibid.

[113] Idrissi, 35.

[114] Ibid.

[115] Dann.

[116] Abdessalami Mubarak, "Moroccan Proverbs," *Abdessalami On Line*, www.angelfire.com/rnb/abdessalami/amthal.html. (accessed February 23, 2006).

[117] Mohamed Ajouaou, "Bestaat De Nederlandse Gastvrijheid?," *Centrum Voor Islam In Europa (c.i.e.)*, March 24, 2003, http://www.flwi.urgent.be/CIE/majouaou4.htm. (accessed February 20, 2006).

Use Friendship Well

Having reliable friends is essential for our well-being, but Proverbs warns us to not demand too much of our friend (Proverbs 25:17). Friendship ripens through discreet sensitivity, to allow space for the other person, because without this the friendship can be harmed. It is compared with eating too much honey (25:16). The following Moroccan proverb, expressing the same truth, has linked both verses together: *If your brother is honey, don't eat him all.*[118]

True Friendship Can Be Painful

According to Proverbs 27:6, a friend is always honest when he rebukes his friend, even if it seems harsh, for the intention is the positive benefit of the other. The errant friend should therefore receive this rebuke with gratitude, realizing its value. The theme of reproof as an element of love also occurs in the following proverbs:

A stone from the hand of a friend is an apple.[119]

The quarrel of lovers is the renewal of love.[120]

Praise your friend before others, but tell him his faults face to face.[121]

Choose your Friends Carefully

Both the book of Proverbs (27:17) and Moroccan proverbs realize the enormous influence the people we associate with can have on our behavior:

Do as your friend does, or leave him.[122]

The one I see you with I take you to resemble.[123]

Realizing the truth that we often start doing what our friends, the people we associate with do, we should *Choose the neighbor before the house, and the companion before the road.*[124] And *Wear what's your size, and mix with your type.*[125] And realize that: *A bull plows only with its equal.*[126]

---

[118] Westermarck.

[119] Ibid.

[120] *World Of Quotes*, "16 Sayings For Moroccoan Proverbs," www.worldof quotes.com/proverb/Moroccan/ (accessed January 20, 2006).

[121] Dann.

[122] Westermarck.

[123] Dann.

[124] Westermarck.

[125] Dann.

[126] Idrissi, 38.

Proverbs continually warns us not to associate with certain kind of people: sinners (1:10-14); wicked, evil men (4:14, 15; 24:1, 2); fools (13:20; 14:7); proud people (16:20); violent men (16:29); hot-tempered men (22:24, 25); drunkards and gluttons (23:20, 21); thieves (29:24) because they will entice us and encourage us to do as they do. On the other hand: "He who walks with the wise grows wise" (13:20).

Also Moroccan proverbs express the truth that a person who is with bad people learns from them what is bad:

He who mixes with the blacksmith gets from him his dirt.[127]

He who goes round with the spice merchant smells of his aroma.[128]

Keep away from quarrelsome people, lest evils should overcome you.[129]

Anyone who makes the crow his traveling companion, he will take him by the carrion.[130]

We played with dogs, and woke up being their cousins.[131]

Mix with the chaff and you will be eaten by the chicken.[132]

Friendship with the mice —whoever wants it should not complain if they eat his flour.[133]

What is mixed with the bran will be eaten by the dogs.[134]

Proverbs 26:17 clearly warns us that interfering with other people's life can become harmful, even if it's our intention to help. Also the following proverb speaks about those who interfere with other people's affairs, as a result they get bitten, by snakes, that is, they are severely attacked because of their interference:

Do not put your hands in holes so that you will not be bitten by snakes.[135]

In a traditionally hierarchical society such as Morocco, not too much friendliness or familiarity is shown to persons of other classes, for example, a

---

[127] Westermarck.
[128] Dann.
[129] Westermarck.
[130] Dann.
[131] Hargraves, 89.
[132] Abdessalami.
[133] Dann.
[134] Westermarck.
[135] Idrissi, 16.

handshake would be acceptable, but a kiss would not. The proverb underneath offers insight into such a relationship. It expresses the truth also found in Proverbs 29:21, namely: indulge someone beneath you and he'll surely take advantage of it:

If you play with the dog, it will lick your lips.[136]

The Use of the Tongue

In a society in which the written word was not yet the normal means of communication, it is hardly surprising that communication by word of mouth played an extremely important role in daily life as reflected in Proverbs.

Skladny calculated that more than 20 % of all the biblical proverbs in chapters 10:1-22:16 and 25-29 are concerned in one way or another with the spoken word and its power.[137]

Kidner points out that as many as three out of the seven abominations listed in Proverbs 6:16-19 are examples of the misuse of words.[138] It is therefore not an exaggeration to say that the use of the tongue is an important theme in the book of Proverbs.

Also Moroccan culture, particularly the Tamazight element of it, is still predominantly an oral culture and also a culture in which someone's honor must be respected in public, which has enormous implications for the use of one's words.

Words and the Heart

Proverbs teaches that what a man says wells up from what he is. The tongue and the heart are frequently used in parallel. (e.g. 10:20; 12:23; 15:7, 28; 16: 23).

This is also found in the following Moroccan proverb, which, like Proverbs, compares the fool and the wise, as seen in the way they use their tongue:
The heart of a fool is in his mouth, the mouth of a wise man is in his heart.[139]

---

[136] Ibid., 17.

[137] Whybray, Survey, 140.

[138] Kidner, Proverbs, 46.

[139] *One Proverb*, "Proverbs From 'moon Over Morocco'," http://www.onepro verb.net/bwfolder/mombw.html. (accessed February 5, 2006).

Words Can Deceive

You can recognize the character of a person from the way he talks (Proverbs 5:3; 7:5; 26:23, 24-26) and Moroccan proverbs emphasize that flattering words can hide a crooked heart:

The snake is nicely decorated, but its drawback is its mouth.[140]

The oleander is beautiful, but it is bitter.[141]

He's like a hot coal, the ash covers it.[142]

Tooth laughs towards tooth, and in the heart there is deception.[143]

Decorative painting and stinging like a wasp.[144]

He who flatters with laughter wants to see you cry.[145]

An aspect of deceiving is boasting, exaggerating and thereby distorting the truth, this is reflected on in Proverbs (25:15) and also in the following Moroccan proverb:

The funeral procession is magnificent and the corpse is a mouse.[146]

Seemingly innocent people can cause you a lot of harm: *A pool with stagnant water is just the one that swallows people.*[147]

We are reminded that people can be like *A thread of silk, soft but it strangles.*[148]

Gentle Words Have Power

Proverbs (15:1, 4; 25:15) expresses the positive power of a gentle word to persuade or to restrain anger. In Proverbs 16:24, which has found its way into the Body of Moroccan proverbs, the effect of gracious words on the hearer is likened to a honeycomb: *Pleasant words are a honey comb, sweet to the soul and healing to the bones.*[149]

---

[140] Dann.

[141] Ibid.

[142] Ibid.

[143] Westermarck.

[144] Ibid.

[145] *Ask The Econsultant,* "Moroccan Proverbs," http://www.econsultant.com/proverbs/moroccan/index.html. (accessed February 20, 2006).

[146] Dann.

[147] Westermarck.

[148] Dann.

[149] One Proverb.

Also Proverbs 24:26 is quoted as a Moroccan proverb: *An honest answer is like a kiss on the lips.*[150]

Other proverbs advise people to use their tongue gently and sweetly:

He who has no honey in his place should put some on the tip of his tongue.[151]

The polite tongue can suck the lioness breast.[152]

Good speech is balanced, may God be merciful to him whose speech is kind.[153]

Beautify your tongue; you will obtain what you desire.[154]

Speak well in advance, you will not (have to) come back the (same) way (to repeat your request.[155]

Do not correct with a strike that which can be taught with a kiss.[156]

The Tongue Can Be a Dangerous Organ

Proverbs teaches that a tongue not only is able to do a lot of good, bring healing (12:18) and reconciliation (25:15), but also to destroy oneself (10:8, 14; 12:13; 18:7), one's relationships (11:9; 16:28) and even whole cities (11:11). Hurtful words are the reason for wrath and anger (15:1), which in turn lead to strife and quarrels (Prov. 30:32, 33), words of the wicked can cause a violent death (12:6).

The damage caused by the wrong use of the tongue also appears in Moroccan proverbs:

The tongue has no bone yet it crushes.[157]

The evil of a person comes from the tongue.[158]

The wound caused by words is worse that the wound of bodies.[159]

---

[150] Ibid.

[151] Westermarck.

[152] Abdessalami.

[153] Westermarck.

[154] Ibid.

[155] Ibid.

[156] English Proverb Album.

[157] *Tawiza.nl,* "Spreekwoorden," http://tawiza.nl/content/sectie/php?cid=49&secties=cat/ (accessed November 10, 2005).

[158] Westermarck.

[159] Ibid.

A fool's lips bring him strife and invite a beating.[160]

No fire enters the oven except through its mouth.[161]

One of the ways the tongue can be used to injure people is by spreading rumors (Proverbs 11:13; 16:27, 28; 17:9; 18:8; 25:23; 26:20, 21) or insulting and slandering others (10:18; 20:20). Gossip and slandering is considered something wrong in the following Moroccan proverbs:

That one, like a dung beetle he is: say something to him and he rolls it into a ball.[162]

Talking about people is caused by sitting.[163]

Every tale-bearer is saltless; he brings evil on his head.[164]

The wound will heal, and shameful talk will never heal.[165]

He who speaks at the nape of my neck is like him who eats my dung.[166]

Don't speak badly of people; (if you do) evil must overtake you or your children.[167]

The mouths of gun-barrels are better than the mouths of dogs.[168]

The talk of him who slanders people is like mud.[169]

Proverbs (17:4) not only condemns gossiping but also listening to it. This same advice is given in the following proverbs:

Don't let the gossiper deceive you – just as he's slandered me he'll slander you.[170]

What he said to you, he'll say about you.[171]

---

[160] One Proverb.
[161] Westermarck.
[162] Dann.
[163] Ibid.
[164] Westermarck.
[165] Ibid.
[166] Ibid.
[167] Ibid.
[168] Ibid.
[169] Ibid.
[170] Dann.
[171] Ibid.

The Need to Use Our Tongue Wisely

Given the power of the tongue, both to bless and to destroy, it comes as no surprise that Proverbs admonishes us to use our tongue wisely. This means:

a) To think before we speak (15:28; 18:13; 20:25), which is also reflected in the proverbs:

Don't put on the saddle before you've put on the bridle.[172]

If I listen, I have the advantage; if I speak, others have it.[173]

Something that is out of your mouth cannot be undone:

If the shot as gone out it does not come back again.[174]

Whoever has let go of a stone can no longer control it.[175]

b) To keep or guard our tongue (10:19; 13:3; 14:3; 17:28; 21:23; 30:32, 33)

In Proverbs restraint in speech is considered an indication of understanding and prudent behavior. Proverbs 11:12 is literally quoted as a Moroccan proverb:

A man who lacks judgment derides his neighbor, but a man of understanding holds his tongue.

There is a major strand of teaching in Proverbs about the importance of silence, and this is also seen in the following Moroccan proverbs:

Into a closed mouth no fly will enter.[176]

Silence for a year is better than a bad word.[177]

Much talking, and silence is better.[178]

A wise woman has much to say and yet remains silent.[179]

Among walnuts only the empty one speaks.[180]

The biggest nuts are those which are empty.[181]

---

[172] Westermarck.

[173] English Proverb Album.

[174] Dann.

[175] Ibid.

[176] Donald W. Hall, "Anthropod Proverbs", http://entnemdept.ifas.ufl.edu/pro verbs.htm. (accessed September 21, 2005).

[177] Westermarck.

[178] Ibid.

[179] One Proverb.

[180] World of Quotes.

[181] One Proverb.

The village gate can be closed, the mouth of the fool, never.[182]

Silence is wisdom and the source of all wisdom.[183]

If the son of pigeons did not speak, the snake would not come to him pursuing.[184]

Repentance for silence is better than repentance for speaking.[185]

Do not respond to a barking dog.[186]

The Role of Money

Judged by the number of proverbs dedicated to this theme, it is certainly one of the most important in Proverbs. For clarity's sake the subject will be divided into several categories.[187]

Foolish Behavior Leads to Poverty

If wisdom and its associated behaviors lead to riches, it is no surprise that Proverbs also teaches that the reverse is true as well: folly results in poverty. Foolish behavior leading to poverty that can be identified both in the book of Proverbs and in Moroccan proverbs.

Laziness

Proverbs 6:6-11; 10:4,5; 12:24, 27; 15:19; 19:15, 24; 20:4, 13; 22;13; 26:13-15

Too proud to beg and too lazy to work.[188]

The head that has no stimulation had better be cut off.[189]

You're a prince and I'm a prince, so who will drive the donkeys.[190]

Work and you will be strong; sit and you will stink.[191]

To work with Christians is better than to loose (time) by sitting idle.[192]

---

[182] Ibid.
[183] Idrissi, 11.
[184] Westermarck.
[185] Ibid.
[186] Ask the Econsultant.
[187] Cited in Tremper Longman III, 120-130.
[188] Dann.
[189] Westermarck.
[190] Dann.
[191] World of Quotes.
[192] Westermarck.

The choice of the day is its early morning.[193]

Much sleep makes a man contemptible.[194]

The dreaming man makes excuses for his inaction and places a fool's cap on his head.[195]

The head of the idle is Satan's workshop.[196]

You give a command to a donkey and give it to his ears.[197]

Too Much Talk, no Action

Proverbs states that 'mere talk' (14:23) or 'chasing fantasies' (28:19) leads to poverty, we find similar truths expressed in other words in the proverbs:

She who goes from place to place will not spin any wool.[198]

It was chatting that burnt the bread.[199]

As long as the shepherd stands, that's how long he will run.[200]

Careless

Closely related to laziness is the careless attitude, carelessly dealing with what you have, leads to poverty is both the message of Proverbs (24:30-34 and 27:23-27) and the proverb: *All that the camel tilled he stamped on.*[201]

An aspect of carelessness is jumping into action without careful planning (21:5), which a proverb states as: *The donkey has eaten his saddle.*[202]

Overindulgence

Another reason given in Proverbs for poverty is over-indulgence (21:17, 20). Also Moroccan proverbs advise that a person should live according to his means and not bite off more than he can chew or do too much and be content with what you have:

---

[193] Ibid.
[194] Ibid.
[195] One Proverb.
[196] Dann.
[197] http://www.Tawiza.nl.
[198] Dann.
[199] Ibid.
[200] Ibid.
[201] Westermarck.
[202] Dann.

Eating beyond measure makes one a sluggard.[203]

Stretch your leg according to the size of your blanket.[204]

Make your mouthful as big as your mouth.[205]

He wants to be a raisin; he's not yet an unripe grape.[206]

Warning about people who want to perform two tasks at the same time that such a thing cannot be performed successfully:

One cannot hold two watermelons in one hand.[207]

Two partridges cannot be caught with a single hand.[208]

Manage with salt and butter until God brings the jam.[209]

Don't twist a rope in the mouth of a calf.[210]

Oppression and Injustice

Sometimes is it not so much foolish behavior of the individual that leads to his or her poverty, but that of others, particularly authorities above them through their oppression and injustice. This is a truth that both the book of Proverbs (13:23; 22:16) as well as Moroccan proverbs knows about: *The sheep of a poor man pasture on the border.*[211]

The Wealth of Fools Will not Last

Although foolish behavior can make someone poor, this doesn't mean that all people that act foolishly are poor. E.g. lazy people can inherit a fortune from their hard-working parents, as stated by the following proverb: *The lion breaks to pieces, and the jackal eats.*[212]

Proverbs (21:6; 22:16) is aware of the fact that wealth can be accumulated by unethical means, but if one is a fool, wealth will inevitably harm its owner, a truth also found in the proverbs:

---

[203] Westermarck.
[204] Dann.
[205] Ibid.
[206] Ibid.
[207] One Proverb.
[208] Idrissi, 16.
[209] One Proverb.
[210] Westermarck.
[211] Ibid.
[212] Ibid.

He who steals a candle must dig a well to hide it in.[213]

The adulterer fears for his wife, and the thief for his house.[214]

Those with Money Must Be Generous

Proverbs urges people to be generous (3:27, 28; 11:24). Because the giving of alms is one of the five duties of Islam it is no surprise that there are several Moroccan proverbs encouraging people to be generous e.g.: *Give what is in your pocket, God will bring you what is absent.*[215]

The truth of Proverbs (11:17) that kindness and cruelty bring their own rewards, is also reflected in the proverb: *The niggard is niggardly with regard to himself, and the money of the generous one will come back to him.*[216]

Wisdom is Better than Wealth

Proverbs leaves us in no doubt that wealth is better than poverty, but also states that it is not the ultimate good. Inner peace (15:6); godliness (16:8); loving (15:17) and peaceful relationships (17:1); wisdom (16:16); honesty (19:22; 28:6) and integrity (19:1) and a good reputation (22:1) are more important than money. Also in Moroccan proverbs the relative value of wealth is emphasized and the following matters are considered more valuable:

Integrity

Better a handful of dried figs and content with that, than to own the gate of peacocks and be kicked in the eye by a broody camel.[217]

Better a piece of bread than honey (which) flies have visited.[218]

Allah may love a poor man, but not a dirty one.[219]

Peaceful Relationships

A peace of bread with union in peace is better than a lamb stake and quarrel.[220]

---

[213] Dann.

[214] Ibid.

[215] Westermarck.

[216] Ibid.

[217] Dann.

[218] Ibid.

[219] One Proverb.

[220] Babette Wagenvoort, "Nieuwe Nederlandse Spreekwoorden", http://www.nieuw enederlandsespreekwoorden.nl/index2.html. (accessed November 15, 2005).

Good Health
Little with health is better than much with sickness or affliction.[221]

To suffer damage in goods is better than in bodies.[222]

A Good Reputation
Respect with little is better than much with disgrace.[223]

A good name is more valuable than a velvet garment.[224]

Usefulness
A brick in a wall is worth more than a pearl on a string.[225]

Wealth has limited value

Proverbs is aware of the fact that wealth not only brings advantages but also trials, which is also expressed in the proverbs:

Abundance of money is a trial for a man.[226]

Owner of a mill, a watered garden and a second wife: not one night does he spend in peace.[227]

One of these trials is false friends (14:20; 19:4, 6), who come to you because of your wealth not because of who you are: *Muzunas make friends and bring the distant one near.*[228]

He who has gold is loved, even if he is a dog, son of dogs.[229]

O you who have money, be a jackal so that they do not put you (i.e. your money) into the pocket and (then) there is no friend.[230]

To the dog that has money, men say: my lord dog.[231]

Respect goes to richness not to people.[232]

---

[221] Westermarck.
[222] Ibid.
[223] Ibid.
[224] Ask the Econsultant.
[225] Dann.
[226] World of Quotes.
[227] Dann.
[228] Westermarck.
[229] Ibid.
[230] Ibid.
[231] English Proverb Album.

He who has money is loved, even though he is bad, the poor one is hated, even though he is god.[233]

Proverbs is quite clear about the fact that riches won't help you on the day of judgment (11:4) and this is also reflected in the proverb: *The grave clothes have no pockets.*[234]

Conclusion

In this chapter more than hundred Moroccan proverbs have been compared with hundred and thirty two verses from the book of Proverbs. We need to understand that there are thousands of Moroccan proverbs that have not been mentioned above. It might be of interest to do a more in-depth study of these and to compare them with the more than 915 verses (about 500 proverbs) in Proverbs. No doubt, such a study would show similarities as well as differences and contradictions between the two.

What the comparisons in this chapter have shown is that the content of Proverbs in several key areas of life often closely resembles, sometimes even to the point of being almost identical in wording, what's expressed in Moroccan proverbs.

Harun Yahya, a pen name used by Mr. Adnan Oktar, a prominent Turkish Muslim intellectual, who has published a book on Solomon, quotes another 103 verses from the book of Proverbs, he believes are compatible with Qur'anic moral values.[235]

This should encourage Christians to freely use Proverbs in sharing the truth of the Bible with their Moroccan friends, realizing that the truth expressed in it, resembles values that are also expressed in the Moroccan. Can it be that some Moroccan proverbs exemplify God's common grace at work, preparing the way for His special grace, fully revealed in Christ Jesus?

---

[232] *School Zonder Racisme*, "Schoolpartnerschappen Vlaanderen Marokko," http://schoolzonderracisme.be/marokko/intercult/marcopolo/marcospreek.htm. (accessed Deceber 21, 2004).

[233] Westermarck

[234] Dann.

[235] Oktar mentions the following 108, five of which are included in this chapter: 1:24-33; 2:10-15, 20-22; 3:5-10, 27-35; 4:14-16, 18.19; 8:1-21; 9:10-12; 10:9; 11:1-8; 12:2, 5, 7, 21, 25; 13:10, 13; 15:1; 16:20; 19:11, 20; 22:1, 2, 4, 5, 16-18; 23:15-19; 22, 23; 24:19, 32; 25:28; 27:1; 28:3, 13, 14, 26, 27; 29:10, 11 http://www.harunyahya.com/books/faith/solomon/solomon.php date posted: February 22, 2006

Chapter 4

The Gospel according to the Book of Proverbs

Introduction

If we had only the book of Proverbs to give to our Muslim friend, how would we help him to understand the essential Biblical doctrines about God, human nature, salvation and especially, the person of Christ? What particular verses would be good bridges to presenting the Muslim with the way, the truth and the life of God in Jesus Christ?

From the beginning of time, when God called: "Adam, where are you?", until the present day, our heavenly Father is actively involved in the redemption of His creation. In the Old Testament God and his redemptive purpose in history are revealed to us in many and various ways. In the lives of people like Abraham, Moses, and David, in the Ten Commandments and other laws that He gave His people, in the institution of the tabernacle and temple with their sacrificial system and priesthood, in the way God dealt with His people Israel and in the words He commanded the prophets to speak on His behalf, God manifested Himself for the redemption of the world. In the New Testament God revealed himself supremely in His Son who took up in himself all of these strands of Old Testament revelation and wove them into a perfect picture of the deity. He was the ultimate radiance of God's glory of which the earlier revelations were shadows. He was the exact representation of God's being, towards which the rest of the Bible points.

After his resurrection Jesus explained to two of His disciples "what was said in all the Scriptures concerning Himself" (Luke 24:27). And a little later he said to a broader group of His disciples: "Everything must be fulfilled that is written about me in the Law of Moses, the Prophets and the Psalms" (Luke 24:44).

The fact that Proverbs is given a place in the canon means that it was recognized that it contains revelation of God which is authentic and in line with the rest of Scriptures, which can "make one wise for salvation through faith in Jesus Christ" (2 Timothy 3:15). And as part of the Scriptures, it is included in Jesus' comments above. Ultimately He is the One who gives meaning to the message of Proverbs.

Jesus and the Book of Proverbs

Jesus grew up in a Jewish setting and was familiar with the religious books of the Jews, which we find in the Old Testament. He used the Scriptures to justify his actions and often referred back to what God had revealed to His people in the past.

Jesus identified Himself with the wisdom as found in Proverbs in the following ways.

Comparing Himself with Solomon

His words in Luke 11:31:"The Queen of the South will rise at the judgment with the men of this generation and condemn them; for she came from the ends of the earth to listen to Solomon's wisdom, and now one greater than Solomon is here," seem to make clear that the wisdom of the Old Testament so imperfectly manifested in the character and teachings of Solomon, is now perfectly revealed in the matchless life and words of Him, who is David's greater son.

Identifying Himself with Wisdom's Zealous Invitation

In Proverbs 9:1-5, Woman Wisdom is preparing a feast to which people are invited. After the meal has been prepared and the table set, she sends out her helpers to invite people to come and eat of her bread and drink of her wine. Elsewhere in Proverbs (1:20ff. and 8:1ff.) we see Wisdom's evangelistic zeal. She cries aloud in the street, in the market place, at the gate and from the top of high places, so that all may hear it. She brings her message to the people and to the places where they are.

> Our Lord, in whose life that divine wisdom became supremely manifested followed the same pattern of evangelism, going about among the people, preaching from the hillside, lake, and crowded market place imparting the words of life to those who would hear; and when he wanted to impress upon his hearers the importance of this kind of work, he could find no better image than that used by wisdom of old: a sumptuous feast to which all are invited by the messengers as they cry: "Come, eat my food, and drink the wine I have mixed" (Proverbs 9:5; Matthew 22:4).[236]

His Association with Woman Wisdom

In Matthew 11, Jesus addresses opponents who argued that John the Baptist was ascetic in his lifestyle, while Jesus was too celebratory. In response to this, Jesus said: "For John came neither eating nor drinking, and they say, 'He has a demon.' The Son of Man came eating and drinking, and they say, 'Here

---

[236] Fritsch, 173.

is a glutton and a drunkard, a friend of tax collectors and sinners.' But wisdom is proved right by her actions." (Matthew 11:18, 19). Tremper Longman III concludes, "In that last sentence, Jesus claims that his behavior represents the behavior of Woman Wisdom herself."[237]

His Use of Parables

Jesus' most characteristic form of teaching was the parable. This usually was part of the repertoire of the wisdom teacher. The Hebrew word for 'proverb' (*mashal*) was translated into the Greek word "parable" (*parabole*). Tremper Longman III therefore concludes: "It is not stretch to say that Jesus was a first century wisdom teacher."[238]

Basing His Teaching on Words and Ideas from Proverbs

Jesus based several of his teachings on words and ideas from Proverbs.[239] Some motifs from the Old Testament proverbs are paralleled in some of the parables of Jesus.

The Parable of Two Foundations

Jesus' parable on the wise and foolish builders in Matthew 7:24-27 seems to be inspired by the words of Proverbs 10:25 and Proverbs 12:7.

The Parable of the High and Low Places

It seems very likely that the words of Proverbs 25:6, 7 were in the mind of Jesus when he spoke the parable in the Pharisee's house, recorded in Luke 14:7-11: "Do not exalt yourself in the king's presence, and do not claim a place among great men; it is better for him to say to you, 'Come up here,' than for him to humiliate you before a nobleman."

The Parable of the Rich Fool

Jesus' parable of the rich man and his barns (Luke 12:16-21) was probably based on a thought expressed in Proverbs 27:1.

The Parable of the Friend at Midnight

In Jesus' teaching on prayer in Luke 11, he uses a parable of someone who receives a friend and midnight and who goes to his neighbor to lend some bread. Jesus' lesson that the neighbor will give the bread, despite the inconvenient time of the day, reflects the truth of the words of Proverbs 3:28.

---

[237] Tremper Longman III, 107.

[238] Ibid.

[239] A lot of what's mentioned here is taken from the article of Fritsch.

Other Teachings of Jesus Based on Words and Ideas from Proverbs

The Use of the Tongue

As we have already seen in the chapter four, Proverbs has a lot to say about the tongue and the lips and the power that lies in them. Proverbs 18:21 says: "The tongue has power over life and death." Jesus seems to echo this same thought in Matthew 12:36, 37.

The Importance of Humility

In his teaching on humility (Luke 14:11; 18:14) Jesus says: "For everyone who exalts himself will be humbled, and he who humbles himself will be exalted." He uses almost the same words as found in Proverbs 29:23: "A man's pride brings him low, but a man of lowly spirit, gains honor."

The Importance of a Pure Heart

In Proverbs 4:23 we are encouraged: "Above all else, guard your heart, for it is the wellspring of life." In his teaching on purity Jesus also emphasized the pureness of heart as compared to becoming unclean by eating certain kind of food (Matthew 15:18-20).

Trusting God for the Right Thing to Say

In Proverbs 16:1 we read: "To man belong the plans of the heart, but from the Lord comes the reply of the tongue." This thought fits in well with Jesus' encouragement to His disciples to not worry about what to say or how to say it. "At that time you will be given what to say, for it will not be you speaking, but the Spirit of your Father speaking through you" (Matthew 10:19, 20).

His Teaching on Giving

In what Jesus says on giving in Matthew 5:42, "Give to the one who asks you, and do not turn away from the one who wants to borrow from you," he closely resembles the words of Proverbs 3:28: "Do not say to your neighbor, "Come back later; I'll give it tomorrow" – when you now have it with you."

His Teaching on Richness

When Jesus says in Matthew 6:19: "Do not store up for yourselves treasures on earth, where moth and rust destroy, and where thieves break in and steal," we can hear echo's of the words found in Proverbs 11:4 and Proverbs 11:28.

His Teaching on Recompense

Proverbs 14:31 and 19:17 may provide the basis for Jesus' teaching that whatever we do for those in need, we do for Him (Matthew 25:31-46).[240]

---

[240] Eldon Woodcock, *Proverbs: A Topical Study* (Grand Rapids, Michigan: Zondervan Publishing House, 1988), 79.

His Teaching on how to Deal with Our Enemies

Jesus' teaching in the Sermon on the Mount on how to relate to our enemies, resemble the exhortations in Proverbs with regard to the relationship to one's enemy as found in the following verses: Proverbs 20:22; 24:17, 18; 24:28, 29; 25:21, 22.

To the list above, we could add other examples, such as his teaching on the poor in spirit (Matthew 5:3 and Proverbs 16:19); his teaching on honoring one's parents (Matthew 15:4, 6 and Proverbs 28:24); and his teaching on the merciful (Matthew 5:7 and Proverbs 11:17).

Finding Gospel Bridges in Proverbs

As we have seen Jesus appeared to base several of his teachings and parables on the truth found in Proverbs and He identified Himself with the wisdom found in this book. This gives us confidence that it is legitimate to look at it from the other side, that is, to explore what verses and concepts in the book of Proverbs might be best used to point someone to Jesus and to stimulate the desire in someone's heart for the ultimate expression of God's Wisdom: the Son of God, the Savior of the world.

We could look for isolated verses that point to some truth that is expressed in the life and work of the Lord Jesus Christ. For example, many have seen in the question asked in Proverbs 30:4: "What is His name, and the name of His son?" as a prophetic reference to God's revelation of "a Son". Other verses that could be used as discussion starters with Muslims are: Proverbs 10:2, 16:6 and 28:13.

Despite the value of using verses such as these, the best Gospel bridge from Proverbs can be found in the metaphor of Woman Wisdom.

Personified Wisdom in Proverbs

In the Old Testament wisdom is usually an abstract quality that can be attributed either to God and man. Only in Proverbs 1-9 it is described as a living person.

Wisdom in Personal Terms

In Proverbs 1-9 there are several verses that represent wisdom in personal, feminine terms. In 3:16 wisdom is said to hold long life, riches and honor in her two hands. In 4:6 the reader is promised that if he loves her she will protect him, and in 4:8-9 that if he embraces her she will exalt and honor him and also place a crown on his head. Whybray comments: "That wisdom is here portrayed as a bride is confirmed by 7:4, where the pupil is urged to say to her, 'You are my sister' (i.e., bride)"[241]

---

[241] Whybray, 72.

In two passages in Proverbs Woman Wisdom speaks in the first person: 1:20-33 and chapter 8. In 1:20-33 Wisdom is personified as a preacher with prophetic gifts. In 8:1-21 she appears as one who makes a general appeal to mankind, and strengthens her appeal by displaying her powers and the gifts which she has to offer. But in 8:22-31 she claims to be the child and beloved of God, one who has observed and actively participated in the acts of creation. She makes this claim in order to show her primordial origin and her closeness to God.

Who or What Does Wisdom Stand for?

The text does not describe a literal Woman Wisdom. So the question remains who does this woman stand for? What is her status? Is she being presented to us as a member of the angelic hierarchy, or only as an idea personified?

Tremper Longmann III believes that the answer to the identity of Woman Wisdom is found in the location of her house in Proverbs 9. "Her house is located in 'the heights overlooking the city' (Proverbs 9:3). Indeed, the Hebrew text stresses that her house is the highest point of the city. Here we need to transport ourselves back into the world of the original text, where we discover that the building on the high point of the city is the temple."[242]

From this he concludes that Woman Wisdom stands for God. "She is a poetic personification of God's wisdom and represents God, as a part for the whole."[243] According to Wicks, wisdom is "a reverential synonym for God, acting on the world and man...simply a periphrasis for God in action."[244] Kidner agrees with the observation that Wisdom is a personification of God's attribute of wisdom: "While some of the language was destined to prepare the way for the New Testament Christology, the portrait in its own context is personifying a concept, not describing a personality."[245]

Tremper Longmann III considers the figure of Woman Wisdom a metaphor for God's relationship with his people, alongside other metaphors, like shepherd, father and king. "These are different manifestations of who God is for his people."[246]

---

[242] Tremper Longman III, 33.

[243] Ibid.

[244] Quoted in James D.G Dunn, *Christology in the Making*; A New Testament inquiry into the origins of the doctrine of the incarnation (Philadelphia: The Westminster Press, 1980), 327.

[245] Kidner, 23.

[246] Tremper Longman III, 33.

Jesus is Presented as the Incarnation of God's Wisdom

When contemplating on the place that Woman Wisdom receives in the Book of Proverbs, as a way of asserting God's nearness, his involvement in His world and his concern for His people, as a reverential synonym for God, as a perfect description of the immanence of God, the reaching out of the exalted God which the wise man experiences here on earth, that which man may know of God and of God's will, it is no wonder that the first Christians identified Christ as Wisdom and that in the New Testament Jesus is presented as the incarnation of God's wisdom. Fritsch states it well: "The early Church Fathers looked upon the sublime personification of wisdom in chapter 8 as one of the clearest pictures of Christ in the Old Testament, and in many instances they used this passage to help formulate their ideas about the Second Person of the Trinity."[247]

Woman Wisdom: a Gospel Bridge?

As mentioned above, in His teaching Jesus regularly uses truths that seem clearly linked with and based upon the wisdom found in Proverbs. He also compares himself with Solomon and his wisdom. When people are confused about his identity he associates himself with Woman Wisdom (Matthew 11:19).

We can identify four parallels between Woman Wisdom and Christ: God acting in creation, God acting in revelation, God acting in salvation and God acting in mediation.

Woman Wisdom and Christ: God Acting in Creation

Being with God before Creation

The matter of the origin of Woman Wisdom is a matter of much debate among scholars. The discussion centers on the word *qanani* in verse 22 and is about whether this word means "God acquired (or possessed) me" or "created me," "brought me forth." It is beyond the scope of this book to address this issue here. What is clear from the passage is that wisdom was with God before creation of the world and mankind.

Tremper Longmann III points to the similarities between the words of 8:22: "The Lord formed me from the beginning (*reshit*)," and the very first verse of the Bible: "In the beginning (*bereshit*) God created the heavens and the earth" (Genesis 1:1). He also sees other connections between Woman Wisdom and creation:

---

[247] Fritsch, 170.

Later, when the poet says 'I was born before the oceans were created,' the word 'oceans'(*tehomot*) echoes *tehom* over with the Spirit of God hovered (Genesis 1:2). The pushing back of the waters and the establishment of their boundaries (Proverbs 8:29) recall the pushing back of the waters to form the dry ground on the third day (Genesis 1:9-13). The parallels go on and on, showing a close connection between Wisdom and creation.[248]

The New Testament clearly points to the fact that Jesus was with God in the beginning. The prologue of John's Gospel resembles with the language in Proverbs 8. The Word of God, which is identified as Jesus was "in the beginning with God" (John 1:2). In Colossians 1:15, the apostle Paul speaks of "Christ as the firstborn over all creation," words that seem to resonate with Proverbs 8:22. "Paul is inviting a comparison: Wisdom was the firstborn in Proverbs 8; Jesus is the firstborn in Colossians."[249] Jesus himself, in a discussion with the Jews about Abraham, clearly points to his pre-existence, when He says: "I tell you the truth, before Abraham was born, I am" (John 8:58).

Agent of Creation

In Proverbs 8:30 Wisdom is presented as the 'architect of God's creation.'[250]

"Wisdom is regarded as closely associated with the Lord and one of his major acts – creation. In this way wisdom is given an enhanced status of supreme importance."[251]

Wisdom played an active role in creation together with the Lord. Proverbs 8:22-36 stresses that God created the cosmos by virtue of his age-old wisdom. In Colossians 1:16 Paul clearly states that by Christ all things were created. According to Dunn: "What means to say that Christ is the creative power (= wisdom) of God by means of which God made the world."[252] Tremper Longman III comments: "Paul is inviting a comparison between Wisdom is the

---

[248] Tremper Longman III, 105.

[249] Ibid.,108.

[250] Scholars are debating the meaning of the word *amon* in Proverbs 8:30. The issue is whether this word means 'a master craftsman or architect', who actively participated in God's creation of the world, or whether the word should be interpreted as 'brought up', referring to wisdom as having been a little child at the time of the creation of the world, which would exclude the notion that she participated actively in the work of creation. It is beyond the scope of this book to address this matter.

[251] Boström, 51.

[252] Dunn, 190.

agent of divine creation in Proverbs and Christ is the agent in Colossians."[253] Also Revelation 3:14 seem to resonate with the ideas behind Proverbs 8:22-30, particularly when it refers to Jesus as 'the ruler of God's creation.' Tremper Longman III thinks that this phrase "may represent the meaning of that difficult word in Proverbs 8:30, the "architect" of creation."[254]

An Intimate Relationship with God

In Proverbs 8:22-31 Woman Wisdom claims to be the child and beloved of God, one who has observed and actively participated in the acts of creation. She makes this claim in order to show her primordial origin and her closeness to God. She says "she always rejoices in the presence of God" (8:30). Also in 8:12 this mutual knowledge of knowing God and being known by God is highlighted. These words seem to come close to what Jesus says in Matthews 11:27: "No one knows the Son except the Father, and no one knows the Father except the Son and those to whom the Son chooses to reveal Him."

Woman Wisdom and Christ: God Acting in Revelation

The burden of Proverbs is that Woman Wisdom actively seeks men rather than being there to be sought. The whole emphasis is on the initiative of God in revealing Himself as Wisdom and, combined with the relating of 'the fear of the Lord' to everyday life. Edgar Jones believes that we find in the book "a preparation of the mind of the nation for the Incarnation of God in Jesus, Word and Wisdom of God."[255] And he is convinced that "the term Wisdom is significant for our thinking about God and especially his relationship with men, that is, as a medium of revelation."[256]

A Zealous Public Ministry

We should ask what effect the exaltation of Woman Wisdom as being as the "firstborn" is bound to produce. Murphy points out: "Is it not true that her kerygmatic stature is considerably heightened? Who can afford not to listen (8:32) to her, in view of her close association with Yahweh? The kerygmatic function of these lines seem quite undeniable."[257] Tuinstra adds that Woman Wisdom's old age legitimizes her message: "Referring to her old age, a very

---

[253] Tremper Longman III, 108.

[254] Ibid.

[255] Edgar Jones, *Proverbs and Ecclesiastes: Introduction and Commentary* (London: SCM Press, 1961), 53.

[256] Ibid., 43, 44.

[257] Roland E. Murphy, "The Kerygma of the Book of Proverbs," *Interpretation* 20 (1966).

special quality, that gives her a smell of godliness, wisdom commends itself to humanity. Wisdom legitimizes herself and she bases this on her being created by God before all times."[258]

In 1:20-33 Wisdom is personified as a preacher with prophetic gifts. She is bold. We find her in the streets, the squares, the city gates. In 8:1, 2 she shouts out from the hilltop near the road and at the crossroads. This is certainly what we find Jesus do. He went through towns and villages, teaching in the synagogues, in houses, in public squares, on hilltops.

Sending out Prophets

Wisdom and Jesus not only share their public prophetic and evangelic ministry, they also have in common that they both send out prophets. In Proverbs 9:3 we read that Wisdom sends prophets while in Matthew 23:34-39 Jesus clearly says that He send out prophets.

Dunn believes that Matthew seems to identify Jesus as Wisdom. He demonstrates this by comparing Wisdom passages in Matthew with their Lukan counterparts. One of these is Matthew 23:34-36 (Luke 11:49-51). In Luke 11:49, we read: "The wisdom of God said: I will send...," while in Matthew 23:34, Jesus says: "I will send..." Dunn concludes: "Matthew has transformed the saying of Wisdom into a saying of Jesus Himself. He has no problem doing this because for him Jesus *is* Wisdom."[259]

Putting Themselves at the Center of the Message

When Woman Wisdom cries aloud in the streets and public places and appeals to man, she doesn't point to someone or something else, but puts herself at center of all the good things she has to offer. This is what Von Radd finds significant: "The most important thing is that wisdom does not turn towards man in the shape of an "It", teaching, guidance, salvation or the like, but in the shape of a person, a summoning "I". So wisdom is truly the form in which Yahweh makes Himself present and in which he wishes to be sought by man."[260]

Dermot Cox points to the fact that wisdom "speaks in her own person with her own authority. The intention is to encourage the pupil to cleave to her, to develop a personal relationship with her."[261]

---

[258] E.W Tuinstra, *Spreuken I* [Proverbs 1] (Baarn: Callenbach, 1996), 203.

[259] Dunn, 202.

[260] Murphy, 13.

[261] O.F.M. Dermot Cox, *Proverbs with an Introduction to Sapiential Books* (Wilmington Delaware: Michael Glazier Inc, 1982), 158.

This is something that is very characteristic of Jesus. Not only was He anointed by God with the Holy Spirit and power and did he go around doing good and healing all who were under the power of the devil, because God was with him (Acts 10:38); not only did He announce the coming of the Kingdom of God, (Mark 1:14, 15), but He boldly said that He is the door into the Kingdom and that one would not enter the Kingdom of God but by Him (John 14:6).

Woman Wisdom and Christ: God Acting in Salvation

Wisdom is seen as sharing in the process of creation and in the redemption of that creation. God is Creator and Redeemer, and these activities are linked in this passage with Wisdom. These verses, emphasizing as they do the choice between life and death that Wisdom offers, point forward to the work of Christ as Word and Wisdom of God in the New Testament. It is Christ who combines in his person the creative and redeeming power of God (John 1:4, 12; 1 Corinthians 1:24, 30).

Offering Nothing Less than Life Itself

Wisdom possesses the authority to boldly claim in Proverbs 8:35: "He who finds me finds life, and obtains favor from Yahweh." This is a remarkable statement and expresses the close relationship between the Lord and Woman Wisdom, because only God can speak in this way. Therefore Murphy concludes that "the kerygma of wisdom can be summed up in one word: life."[262]

The concept of 'life' as found in the book of Proverbs, is quite elastic. It can refer to a long life: sheer existence in many days (3:2, 16; 4:10; 9:11); it can refer to a harmonious family life (15:27); and in 3:22 it seems to speak of vitality of one's whole being. But in several places it is not too much to say that 'life' means fellowship with God, as the second part of Proverbs 8:35 seems to refer to. Kidner also sees this in other verses in Proverbs:

> In Proverbs 19:23, where the parallel to 'life' is the phrase 'shall abide satisfied', we are to understand it in a spiritual rather than a physical sense. This understanding of 'life' as implying more than mere existence is expressed most tellingly in the phrases 'tree of life', 'fountain of life' and 'path' or 'way of life'.[263]

Tree and fountain of life refer to God's sources of renewal, temporal and spiritual, and symbolize the blessings of a right relationship to God. "The metaphors tell their own story, but this is reinforced by the overtones of Gene-

---

[262] Murphy, 9.
[263] Kidner, 54.

sis 2 and 3, where the tree bore the fruit of immortality, and the river watered the garden of God. Tree and river appear in the end-time vision of Ezekiel 47: 1-12 when the glory has returned (cf. Rev. 22:1, 2)."[264]

Although here and there Proverbs seems to provide a glimpse of viewing life as a goal beyond the grave (e.g. 11:7; 12:28; 14:32), life after death, as we now understand it in the light of the New Testament, lies beyond the horizon of Proverbs. Nevertheless, in the book of Proverbs: "Life was a great grace – it was all, and it depended upon one's relationship to the living God."[265]

This understanding was deepened by one who was wiser than Solomon, who said: "And this is eternal life, that they may know thee the only true God, and Jesus Christ, whom thou hast sent" (John 17:3).

Pointing Clearly to the Consequences of Rejection

In Proverbs 1:24-32, Woman Wisdom makes clear what the consequences are for rejecting her and her message. This can be found in Jesus' life too. Like Wisdom is being rejected Christ is being rejected (1 Corinthians 8:6; 10:1ff., Colossians 1) The call of Woman Wisdom to make a choice and the contrast with foolishness, underlines the seriousness of her message. It is a choice between life and death. (1:20-33; 8:2-21; 9:1-6).

Living an Ethical Pure Life

Wisdom is closely associated with righteousness (8:6), truth (8:7), wholesome behavior (8:8) and good judgment (8:12), with common sense, success, insight and strength (8:14, 15). On the other hand, she tells us that she stays as far away as possible from deception, evil, pride and arrogance (8:7, 8, 13). In Matthew 11:19 Jesus says: "But wisdom is proved right by her actions." In this sentence Jesus claims that his behavior represents the behavior of Woman Wisdom herself.

Woman Wisdom and Christ: God Acting in Mediation

Mediator between God and Man

In looking at Woman Wisdom in Proverbs 8 it is important to not only focus on her relationship with God, but also her relationship with and function in the world of human beings. This is especially emphasized in vv. 30-31, where she claims to have "rejoiced in his (God's) created world and delighted in

---

[264] Ibid.
[265] Murphy, 13.

mankind". The picture given of Woman Wisdom in the book of Proverbs is very much that of a mediator between God and man.

> The arrangement in verses 30, 31 clearly shows that there is a dual relationship between (1) wisdom and the Lord, on the one hand, and (2) wisdom and creation and mankind on the other. Wisdom plays before the Lord and is his delight, but she also plays on his earth, the abode of mankind, and her delight is mankind. In a sense, wisdom functions as an intermediary between God and man, between God and his world.[266]

"The personified Wisdom in Proverbs 1-9 is a poetical device employed by the wise to express that wisdom was a mediator of the godly presence, as a means of bringing God and man together."[267]

> Central to a proper understanding of the phenomenon of personification of wisdom is the fact of an abstract name being used. Yahweh is himself wise, and he desires a relationship to man, so His wisdom becomes a dynamic of relationship, and so a person. The personification emphasizes the desirability of wisdom, something that is so personal it must be acquired if one seeks life. Wisdom thus becomes a force in which God makes himself present and in which he wishes to be sought. Proverbs 8:35 shows Wisdom speaking as if she were God. Wisdom is a channel by which God can reach out to humanity, and draw humanity to himself.[268]

Conclusion

Woman Wisdom is presented in Proverbs as an agent of creation that has an intimate relationship with God before the creation of the world; and as a medium of revelation of the true and only God, who actively seeks the wellbeing of men, and who boldly declares to be the centre of salvation, offering nothing less than life itself and thereby carrying out the role of mediator between God and man.

Using this metaphor, Proverbs paints a picture of the life and work of Christ. While Woman Wisdom was never a person of flesh and blood, but only a metaphor, Christ has taken on human nature. It is no exaggeration to say that He is the only person who ever lived, who carried out all that is described in Proverbs of Woman Wisdom.

---

[266] Boström, 55.
[267] Tuinstra, 28.
[268] Dermot Cox, 74.

As we read the description of wisdom in Prov. 8:22-31, we cannot escape the clear teaching that Jesus Christ is the representation of the wisdom of God. "To yield our lives to Jesus Christ is the ultimate act of wisdom. To be in Him is to be in the wisdom of God."[269]

The fact that Woman Wisdom dominates the scene in the first nine chapters of Proverbs and that these first nine chapters are often considered to be the hermeneutical grid through which the rest of the book should be read, give the metaphor of Woman Wisdom a strategic place in the whole book. By listening to her and understanding what and who she represents, we begin to make sense of the hundreds of isolated sayings in the rest of the book.

Over against Woman Wisdom stands Woman Folly. Although she speaks only once, it becomes clear that she is after the same thing that Woman Wisdom is after: the loyalty of men. Both issue an invitation to dine (Proverbs 9:4, 16), which is an invitation to a relationship. "To further understand this rich image, we need to consider more closely the ancient Near Eastern notion that to dine with someone is to enter into a deep and intimate relationship with that person."[270]

Proverbs 1-9 culminates in a choice that the reader must make before proceeding in the book. With whom will you dine, Woman Wisdom or Woman Folly? This is a choice between Yahweh and the false gods of the nations and is a matter of life and death. "Following Folly, results in death (9:18); to dine with Lady Wisdom, however, brings life (1:33; 3:16-18)."[271]

"To embrace Woman Wisdom is to enter a relationship with Jesus Christ."[272]

While this would make this metaphor of Woman Wisdom one of the most powerful Gospel bridges in Proverbs, our Muslim friends need help from Christians to understand this 'hermeneutical grid' as this will not be obvious to them when reading the book of Proverbs or when picking up one of the verses. By helping our Muslim friends understand and embrace Woman Wisdom, we can help them to enter a relationship with Jesus Christ.

---

[269] Jerry Falwell, *Wisdom for Living* (Wheaton, Illinois: SP Publications Inc, 1984), 11.

[270] Tremper Longman III, 35.

[271] Ibid.

[272] Ibid., 110.

Chapter 5

The Book of Proverbs in Christian Witness

Introduction

In answering the question of the value of using Proverbs in sharing the Gospel with Muslims, it is helpful to find out learn how Christians have used this book for such purposes and with what results. Already in 1946 Godfrey E. Phillips wrote:

> In passing, we note here with interest the extraordinary popularity of Proverbs today in many countries where the gospel is preached to non-Christian; it almost appears there to be the best-seller among the scripture portions which are separately sold. Missionaries sometimes deplore this; they would much prefer to sell one of the gospels. But its attractive rhythmical form, its humor, the ease with which it is understood, account for its acceptability, and after all it brings the Jewish Torah, part of divine revelation, into touch with daily life... It may well be that to people whose thoughts of God and of human life have yet to be lifted to the level of those of the Jews, this apparently unevangelical textbook of behavior represents a necessary stage in their preparation for the Gospel.[273]

These words, written more than 60 years ago, should wet our appetite in looking at contemporary examples of the use of Proverbs and local proverbs in sharing the Gospel and survey their successes and failures and lessons that can be learned from that and this is what this chapter is set out to do.

The African Proverbs Project[274]

The African Proverbs Project was designed to promote collection, publication and study of African proverbs with particular attention to their relationship to Christian witness, their role in modern Africa and their significance for a number of academic disciplines.

---

[273] Godfrey E. Phillips, *The Transmission of the Faith* (London: Lutterworth Library, 1946), 29, 30.

[274] *The Wisdom of African Proverbs*, CD-ROM, ed. Dr. Stan Nussbaum, (Colorado Springs: Global Mapping International, 1998).

The Project ran from 1992 to 1996 under the umbrella of two Christian organizations.[275] The rationale behind the project was that although proverbs are the distilled genius of oral cultures, perhaps even an encapsulation of the whole, their potential value for modern thought and life is little recognized. Also, Christian leaders have not yet gone very far toward integrating traditional proverbs with theology in the quest for a genuine African Christian identity and proverbs have not become one of the basic components of theological education. It was felt that through the use of African proverbs, the church, the university and the world would be enriched and also the gospel would be seen to bring more healing and less cultural schizophrenia to Africa.

The project raised the profile of the African proverb through an integrated set of programs including conferences, new publications by commissioned writers, reprints and the development of research tools.

Included in the project is The Proverbs for Preaching and Teaching Series. The purpose of this series was to encourage the use of African proverbs as aids to Christian moral instruction, as textbooks in Bible institutes and seminaries, as well as resources for church leaders. Each book contains an introductory chapter comparing and contrasting the values of African proverbs and the Bible. The body is an explanation of 100 to 200 local proverbs, showing how each could be used in Christian instruction.

The papers that came out of the conferences and several of the works mentioned above, as well as reprints of several classic proverb collections and several recent ones were put on a CD: The Wisdom of African Proverbs. Over 25,000 proverbs from at least 27 different languages were brought together this way. It is hoped that publication on CD will bring this work to the attention of people worldwide, some of whom may be inspired to attempt similar things in other languages.

This project does not include proverbs of Morocco or any other country in North African (north of the Sahara), but underlines the importance of using indigenous proverbs in sharing the Gospel with people, as Joshua N. Kudadjie, series editor on the Proverbs For Preaching and Teaching Series states:

> It is important to note that Jesus Christ ... also used the method of influencing people from the outside by appealing to their minds and hearts through teaching. In doing this, he used stories and proverbial sayings. There can be no doubt, then, that the present-day Church may attain its

---

[275] *Joint Ministry in Africa*, which combines the Africa work of two denominations, the United church of Christ and the Christian Church (Disciples of Christ); and *Global Mapping International*, an independent evangelical organization based in the USA.

goal (which is to make all peoples the followers of Christ and teach them to obey what he has commanded), if it encourages the proper use of proverbial sayings. In using these indigenous proverbial sayings, however, the Church must correct and replace what is not so good in them, and add on from the Scriptures what is more excellent.

The church which has always been interested in people living the morally good life, must use African proverbs even more earnestly, especially in preaching and teaching. Their use will help immensely to teach the truths of many biblical themes and stories, and to affect the moral, social and spiritual lives of the people for the better; for when a proverb is used correctly, it speaks to the intellect, the soul and the heart – that is, to the understanding, the feelings and the will. Over the centuries, African proverbs have successfully done this. They can, thus, be used to great advantage in Christian preaching and teaching.[276]

In his paper 'The use of Biblical Proverbs for the evangelization of Africa', Jan Knappert seeks to answer two questions: 1) Can we use Biblical proverbs for the evangelization of Africa, and if so, how? 2) Can we use African proverbs for that purpose? He concludes:

The only successful, promising or even possible method to influence not only a people's thoughts and motivations but also their customs and daily behavior will be by means of adding hundreds nay thousands of proverbs to the language and anchor them in the minds and memories of the people.

Thus missionaries wishing to convert people must not only speak the people's language but give the people a set of new proverbs to add and hopefully replace unsuitable old proverbs. There are many proverbs in African languages that Christians find offensive. Only proverbs can replace proverbs in the minds of African peoples. Westerners have lost the power of proverbs in their culture, so that they do not appreciate the impact that a series of well-chosen poetic proverbs can have on a captive audience, if produced by an eloquent preacher at the right moments in his sermon. Words have power.

Obviously, a selection is necessary of the proverbs that are suitable for our purpose. This is not a problem in those language areas where the proverbs have been collected ... . It appears that in each of the great language areas of Africa there are thousands of proverbs. Some of those, a few perhaps, can be utilized as they are, for the fortification of Christian concepts,

---

[276] The Wisdom of African Proverbs CD-ROM.

others can be adapted by changing a few words, provided we retain the usually highly literary beauty of African proverbs.[277]

Although the Biblical book of Proverbs does not play a significant role in the project, the three books included in Project's 'Proverbs for Preaching and Teaching Series' each have a chapter on Biblical proverbs, in which they also address the Book of Proverbs. Also, Dr. Laurent Nare, in his paper 'Mossi Proverbs and Biblical Wisdom' says that "African traditional wisdom, especially as expressed in African Proverbs, can be easily related to Old Testament wisdom. Obviously there are differences, but there are striking similarities in form and content between African proverbs and Biblical Proverbs of the Old Testament."[278]

Among the forty GA proverbs of Ghana which Joshua N. Kudadjie annotated, he links three with verses from Proverbs.[279] From the ten DANGME proverbs of Ghana he annotated, he links one with Proverbs.[280] David K. Mphande annotated two hundred TONGA proverbs from Malawi and links thirty of those with the Book of Proverbs.[281]

Project Snowflakes[282]

The Christian agency Kairos International has set up a project called "snowflakes" to help Christians around the world realize a breakthrough for God, causing their land to bear and sprout, by bringing the marvelous knowledge and wisdom of God to people. Kairos International is convinced that God's wisdom, as found in the Book of Proverbs can be used as a bridge in effectively reaching people. According to Rick Leatherwood, director of Kairos International:

> There are many good missionaries on the mission fields of the world today. And there is excellent seed, such as the JESUS film and the New Testament in local languages. But there is also a lot of hard ground. However, when the book of Proverbs is taken out from between Psalms and Ec-

---

[277] Ibid.

[278] Ibid.

[279] Proverbs 15:1; 20:4; 27:6.

[280] Proverbs 27:10.

[281] 1:7, 10-15; 3:7; 4:1; 5:1, 2, 20-24; 6:19 (2x); 7:1 (2x); 9:11; 10:1, 27; 11:2 (2x); 12:27; 13:10, 20 (3x); 14:1-6; 15:19, 27; 16:18 (2x); 16:19; 18:9; 19:15; 22:5, 6, 13; 23:19, 20, 21, 22 (2x); 24:1, 2 (4x), 17-18, 28; 26:24; 27:1, 8, 17; 29:1, 20, 22; 30:17; 31:3, 10, 11.

[282] Rick Leatherwood, "The Wisdom Of God as Revealed In Proverbs," *Kairos International*, http://www.kairos.cc/ (accessed February 28, 2006).

clesiastes and appropriately packaged as its own booklet, God's wisdom is able to function like a plow, breaking up the hardness in an unbeliever's heart and softening it through wisdom, so that the truth of the gospel can penetrate and sprout.[283]

Considering the Book of Proverbs as a plow that can prepare the hearts of people for the Gospel of Jesus Christ, Kairos International is committed to provide Christians around the world with written or audio copies of the Book of Proverbs. At the moment, booklets of Proverbs are being used in twenty seven countries by many different mission agencies, denominations, and individuals.[284]

Leatherwood gives some examples of how God has used this booklet or the audio cassettes:[285]

When a booklet of Proverbs was presented to the President of one Central Asian (Muslim) country, he was so impressed in reading it, that he immediately ordered the book developed into a curriculum to be used in their public school system!

In one country where audiocassettes of Proverbs with excellent indigenous background music are being distributed in the local language, an American missionary got into a taxi that already had the cassette playing. The driver had been given the tape a few days earlier by someone else, and had been listening to it over and over again. He then asked the missionary if this was the word of God. Assured that it was, he said "But this is not trying to force its religion on me." He then asked questions non-stop during the next 20 minutes. When they arrived at the point of destination, the driver turned off the motor and continued the conversation. The missionary was able to share the whole message of Christ. She later said that in all the years she had been working in this particular country, she had never had such a wide-open opportunity to share the gospel.

In India, among the more than 220 million speakers of Bengali, the book of Proverbs is finding a warm welcome. Readers write back saying that whereas previously they had trusted in their knowledge gained at university to get them through life, they now understand that the fear of the Lord is the beginning of wisdom.

---

[283] Leatherwood, Rick, Snowflakes: The Common Ground of God's Wisdom; International Journal of Frontier Missions, volume 19:2, summer 2002.

[284] Ibid.

[285] Ibid.

In receiving a book of Proverbs, a man from Azerbaijan said, "I've heard of Solomon all of my life, but I have never read the words of Solomon."

In one village in Azerbaijan old men sat and read the words of Solomon to one another. Since a number of verses in Proverbs relate to marriage, God's wisdom was consequently read at a wedding. A significant step towards cultivating the climate for a movement has been established in this community. Followers of Christ were subsequently viewed favorably, and all of this came about because ordinary believers are not afraid to hand out Proverbs in an informal, natural, and relaxed way.

The goal of Project Snowflakes is to cover the earth with the wisdom of God, believing this will help bring about the favorable conditions for harvest. "If the saints each gave only five of these booklets away, we would cover the world with the wisdom of God!"[286]

Leatherwood is convinced that

The likelihood of Bibles ever being read by Muslims is almost nil. Why? First of all, a large amount of the Bible's content is not common ground to Muslims, and they have been pre-conditioned through years of indoctrination not to read it. Secondly, the Bible's sheer size is a problem. Except for the odd scholar, Arabs are not ardent readers, especially of a book this big. For the same amount of money it would take to print a few thousand Bibles, we can print 1,000,000 booklets of Proverbs. Such a booklet is small enough that people will read it, and completely inoffensive to the Muslim mind. It is common ground, and will bring immediate blessing to the reader with just a casual reading.[287]

While Kairos International makes no link between the Book of Proverbs and local proverbs, it is obvious that they are convinced of the value of using Proverbs as a means of sharing Christian faith with Muslims. Their particular focus is to make booklets of the Book available in as many languages as possible. Also people can read and download the text in English and Arabic or listen to and download the audio version in Arabic from their website.[288]

---

[286] Ibid.

[287] Ibid.

[288] *Kairos International*, "The Wisdom Of God," www.kairos.cc/ (accessed February 20, 2006).

La Red Business Network

LaRed International, an organization that is bringing about global transformation by teaching Kingdom business principles to leaders throughout the world has produced a 40-page booklet entitled *Wisdom for Today's Leaders from the Book of Proverbs.*

In it they have divided verses from the Book of Proverbs into four sections: (1) Business and Leadership; (2) Understanding People; (3) Dealing with Self-Control; (4) Wisdom.

Each section has a great number of divisions about issue related to the subject of that particular section, e.g. honesty, motivating people, laziness, wives, pride, lust, and promises to the wise. Individual proverbs are selected in according with the subject matter they address.

In the forward of this booklet, Bernie Torrence, executive director of La Red Business Network writes:

> Many of you have been seeking a plan for success in your life. This booklet will build you from the inside out rather than simply create an illusion of confidence. These are God's laws for success... Success not only in the business world but also in personal areas such as family, friends and finances. These principles reveal nuggets of truth valuable in all forms of human relations. You will find in this booklet that success is not necessarily measured in riches or fame, but in peace of mind and in fulfillment.... The children of Israel wandered for forty years in the wilderness even though the journey should have only taken eleven days. If they had understood these Proverbs, their journey would have been much shorter. In the next forty pages you will find that wisdom is a spirit, a gift from God that will help you say and do the right thing at the right time. This is a booklet of overcoming. It has made its way into the hearts of people around the world. Some of the principles have been translated into five languages. I guarantee that if you will commit yourself to these practical principles, this booklet will change your life – it changed mine. Our entire company was transformed because of our change in thinking. King Solomon wrote his experiences as he found them. These writings are not a philosophy, but are God's wisdom for living. When you seek wisdom you will find the Kingdom of God. [289]

---

[289] The booklet can be ordered and/or downloaded from the website of LaRed *Lared Business Network*, www.lared.org/ (accessed February 20, 2006).

Although the tone of the introduction gives the impression that Proverbs is a formula for a happy, successful life, this booklet has been used, apparently fruitfully, by Christian business men to help business people in the Muslim world understand Biblical ethics of Business.[290]

India

Singh in India started using the book of Proverbs in his contact with Muslims, because he dealt with people who are negative to other religions and feel their religion is the best one and therefore do not like to know about other religions.

> Their minds are preoccupied with negative thought. In that context if we give them a portion of Bible they will not read it. Proverbs does not speak about any specific religion but gives a practical knowledge for all class of people. Once they read the book of proverbs they become interested to know more about the continuation of such type of literature. We get very good response not only from Muslims but as well as from other non-Christians. I have added several questions at the end of the booklet which have been taken from the context. I want the readers to read it carefully in order to answer the questions. Many have responded how much they have been blessed by reading the booklet. Even some lawyers wrote that they read it daily to get practical knowledge. Most of the churches and organizations are using Proverbs now.[291]

Indonesia

A team of Christian workers that published a contextualized NT in Indonesia, is working on the Old Testament. While waiting for the OT to be finished, they decided to publish the book of Proverbs separately, because "it is a good entry book and can introduce folks, who previously have never read anything, to the holy books."[292]

They published it with a very nice introduction, tying it into history, Indonesian proverbs and literature. It was presented as an attractive and expensive book. They choose to publish the book through a secular publisher and not through the Bible Society as that would have placed it in the "Christian" sec-

---

[290] Information obtained from a former colleague in 2004, who attended a Christian Business Conference in UK in March 2004, during which she was informed about the use of this booklet in the Muslim world.

[291] A. Singh in a personal letter to the author on August 21, 2004 in response to the question how the book of Proverbs is used in India.

[292] E. M., a Christian in Indonesia, in a personal letter to the author on September 14, 2005.

tion of the bookstores where few people ever go (only Christians). By working through a secular/Islamic publisher the book was allowed to be put in the general section and sometimes even Muslim sections of the bookstores.

In October 2004, the book hit the best seller list in bookstores in Indonesia after just 3 months on the shelves, becoming so popular that it drew the fire of a radical Islamic magazine.

> We have sold about 7000 copies and it is going into its next printing. It has given Christian workers a lot of courage and is used as a gift very often. We were going to do advertisements etc but our national colleagues got cold feet and decided not draw too much attention but instead let the Proverbs spread by word of mouth.[293]

As a result many Muslims are reading Scripture for the first time in their lives. "One community chief asked me for a copy after he saw our team reading it after the Tsunami."[294]

The workers decided to not do a mass distribution of the book, because they did not want to draw the attention of extremists. "The biggest success is to see Christian workers have the boldness to give something out to their friends and neighbors. We don't see Proverbs as the end but simply as one more step in the process."[295]

Mali

A Christian working in Mali started collecting local proverbs out of personal interest. He writes:

> Before too long I saw that these proverbs had incredible emotive value to the people – and that even I as a foreigner could evoke strong reactions by quoting a proverb – everything from glee and joy to shame and hurt. They are powerful little bomb shells hat encapsulate the deeply grained world view of the people. I called them "bullets" – they are small but aerodynamic and powerful. So I started using proverbs in the literacy work and they were very successful. I think that the traditional proverbs hold greater weight for a lot of people than the majority religion – which is kind of nice – i.e. being able to talk in depth about heart issues and bypassing the 'religious' debates.[296]

---

[293] Ibid.
[294] Ibid.
[295] Ibid.
[296] A.S. in a personal letter to the author on May 6, 2004.

In Kurdistan, Malaysia and Nigeria the believers and the Muslims really like distributing the booklet of Proverbs in their own language, but it's too early in the process to be able to report on the results.[297]

Arab World

While we've seen that Proverbs is used widely in several Muslim countries around the world, for the purpose of this book it is important to learn more about its use in the Arab world and particularly North Africa, and even more specifically, the country of Morocco.

A Christian media organization has begun filming a new series of thirteen, half hour dramas combining Proverbs with common proverbs found within Arab society. Each episode will have a specific topic. The starting point is a short Arabic proverb illustrated by a conflict between the members of a modern family. This conflict is solved in a creative way by the main character, Goha. Goha is a famous traditional character well known and popular in the whole of the Arab World. He is somehow stupid, but wise and funny as well. From Goha's intervention the viewers will be led to the corresponding Biblical proverb and the Christian view on the situation.[298] The proverbs being used in the episodes are successively: Proverbs 17:1; 26:18; 27:4; 26:11; 23:7; 28:13; 6:6; 18:12; 24:29; 15:27 (2x); 17:22.

Tunisia

For ministry among Muslims in Tunisia, Proverbs is not seen as a priority.

I have not seen interest in the use of the Book of Proverbs in Tunisia. Looking at the Translations Report on Colloquial Versions, in the 11 language group projects, there is no translation of Proverbs. I am not sure what this means, except that for some reason the Proverbs are not selected as a priority. This may reflect the point of view of the western agencies more than the locals, but that would need to be tested. Arabs do like proverbs and use them much more frequently than in the West.[299]

---

[297] Rick Leatherwood in a personal letter to the author on July 2, 2005.

[298] From a personal letter to the author from G.M., the Egyptian scriptwriter, on December 30, 2005.

[299] From LH, a Christian in Tunisia in a personal letter to the author on February 10, 2004.

Morocco

In Morocco on the other hand, some Christians keenly believe in the use of Proverbs, as well as local indigenous proverbs, as becomes clear from a letter, written by a Christian in Morocco:

> Shortly after I arrived in Morocco, I was profoundly influenced by an article in which the author argued for the fact that imagery is powerful and often more effective than concept thinking. He, and other articles following his, bemoaned that fact that the use of proverbs is largely a thing of the past in Western Societies. He further argued, that while educated people tend to believe that they think in logical concepts, even the education person needs and uses imagery more than s/he realizes. This article was a pivotal event for me, and I started making it a goal to seek and use imagery. Later I read James Haldane's book, THE ROMANCE OF MOROCCO. After 40 years of preaching the Gospel in Morocco, he noted: "It is impossible to hook a Muslim on the horns of an argument, but if you find a good story, it is as good as proof to a Muslim."

> I have made it my point to pay attention to proverbs – and so far as is possible – to memorize them. The best proverbs often come from their own culture, because they already know them and their application. So with a sentence or two one hits the nail of truth home.

> Of course, we should use Biblical proverbs. They're God's truth. So they hit home. Incidentally, some Biblical proverbs, I heard on the street in Algeria, before I noted them in the Bible. ("He who digs a hole for his neighbor will fall into it." and "A neighbor who lives close to you is better (more useful) than a brother who lives at a distance.") However, I see no point in first trying to show people that the proverb is from the Bible, before I use it. Often it's appropriate to just quote the proverb, whether Biblical or from local culture, and let it do its work, or as Paul did in Titus 1:12 when he picked up a local proverb and nailed them with it. As the pastor said to the lady who asked him, "How can I quote the Bible when my neighbor says she doesn't believe it?", his response, "The Word of God is a sword and it will cut, whether or not your friend believes it is a sword! Just use it. And it will do its work!"[300]

Another missionary in Morocco writes he does not use Proverbs in evangelistic situations, although he uses Moroccan proverbs quite a lot: "They are great conversation starters and they channel conversations into ethical rather than theological directions, so that we are talking about the real spiritual felt-

---

[300] C.H. in a personal letter on April 7, 2004.

needs of people rather than their theoretical objections to our beliefs."[301] Re-
flecting on linking the Biblical proverbs with Moroccan proverbs, he writes:

> You may find some significant differences between the very active ex-
> hortations in the Biblical Proverbs and the rather more passive and cynical
> observations in the general corpus of Moroccan proverbs. The latter are
> also, to my mind, less abstract and far more picturesque in their imagery,
> and my impression is that Moroccan Christians find the Biblical book a lit-
> tle insipid by comparison. Perhaps it should be called "Exhortations" rather
> than "Proverbs" (Its Arabic title, "Amtal", literally means "metaphors" or
> "similes", which is a bit misleading).[302]

Conclusion

It seems that Proverbs which was a best-seller in 1946 in many countries
where the gospel was preached to non-Christians, has been re-discovered by
many Christians in the late 20th , early 21st century as a way to communicate
God's truth, particularly to Muslims. Those who are using Proverbs experience results much like those of more than 50 years ago, particularly in India,
Indonesia, Kurdistan, Malaysia and Nigeria.

Also, Christians in several countries, including the Arab world, acknowledge the importance of using proverbs, whether biblical or local as conversation starters or to nail home a certain truth with one sentence and while others
use Proverbs to communicate Kingdom business principles to leaders
throughout the world.

Using Proverbs as an evangelism tool is becoming more popular, but to
link local proverbs with Proverbs is not as widespread yet. The biggest excep-
tion is the Proverbs in Africa project, which seeks to integrate traditional
proverbs with theology in the quest for a genuine African Christian identity
and to use proverbs as one of the basic components of theological education.
The results of seems very promising. Another example is the production of a
series of television programs linking Biblical proverbs with local Arabic
(Egyptian) proverbs. As the programs have not been broadcasted, nothing can
be said about the results yet.

---

[301] R.D. in a personal letter on August 29, 2004.
[302] Ibid.

Chapter 6

Summary, Conclusions and Recommendations

Summary

Within Moroccan culture, both among Arabs as well as Berbers, proverbs oil the wheels of the social machine and function as a strong moralizing device. This popularity of proverbs is not only due to the oral character of the Berber languages and the high percentage of Moroccan illiterates, but also to the high respect given to the past and to the importance of respecting someone's honor and dignity. The fact that indirect speech is considered a high value and very polite makes a proverb and excellent tool to communicate truth without offending the person you're speaking with.

While on the one hand the increase of literacy and education leads to a to decrease of the use of proverbs among second and third generation, on the other hand a renewed interest in the Tamazight culture and its various expressions, indicates that proverbs continue to play an important role among the Moroccan (and Muslim) community in Europe.

Proverbs has several features that seem to make it a good evangelistic tool:

- Its lack of references to historical accounts and traditions related to the people of Israel, and only a few references to its religious life.
- Its focus on individuals and their concerns without restrictions to specific national affiliations.
- Its universal content, that is applicable to all people at any period in history.
- Its inclusion of well-known concepts and expressions from the surrounding world, including proverbs of two early Arab converts.

The majority of the Muslim community in Europe has a weak socio-economic status. They are poorly educated, unemployed or working in low-income jobs, speak the European languages poorly and are mainly focused on their own group. For the past 30 years, European Muslim citizens descent and 'indigenous' Europeans generally have not associated socially and this hardly seems to improve among those of the second generation. Exceptions are found in the area of cultural expressions, such as music, art, fashion, film, drama, and writings. These provide bridges between the two communities because they use familiar and cherished aspects of each culture.

When we compare Moroccan proverbs with verses from Proverbs we find many that are very similar in content and sometimes wording. Muslim scholars agree that many verses from Proverbs are compatible with the moral values of the Qur'an.

Jesus clearly identifies Himself with the wisdom as found in Proverbs and bases several of his teachings on words and ideas from the book of Proverbs. The metaphor of Woman Wisdom, that plays a prominent role in the first nine chapters of the book, can be paralleled to Jesus Christ in four ways: God acting in creation, revelation, salvation and mediation.

The use of indigenous proverbs and/or the book of Proverbs in sharing the Biblical truth has been rediscovered during the past twenty years by several churches and Christian organizations. Christians working in sub-Saharan Africa have found that incorporating indigenous proverbs in their preaching and teaching has helped to inculturate the Christian faith. Christians in several Muslim countries have begun distributing copies of Proverbs in local languages with very positive results.

Conclusions

As was said in the introduction, the purpose of this book is to demonstrate whether, and if so in what way, the book of Proverbs can be used to share the Gospel with Muslims. Based on the information gathered, it is fair to conclude that for several reasons Proverbs can indeed be a valuable tool in evangelizing Muslims:

Its Imaginary Style Fits the Oral Relational Worldview of the Moroccans and Other Muslims in Europe.

There are basically two communication processes by which people learn. One method is oral communication which used stories and symbols as the vehicle of conveying ideas, concepts, facts and information. The second method of communication is the literary method used by word cultures which transmit information by means of logically developed, systematically and sequentially outlined and organized summaries or lessons drawn from events, information and data. The people who come under one type or the other are very different in the way they hear, learn or process and transmit information about the world in which they live. It is vital that the method of communicating the Gospel corresponds with the way in which the target people learn and transmit information.[303]

---

[303] Jim Slack, "Western Analytical Cultures Vs. Oral Relational Societies," *The Strategic Network*, 2004, http://www.newway.org/strategy_network/western_ analytical_vs_oral_cultures.htm. (accessed February 27, 2006).

Many Muslims in Europe come from an oral culture, and although the future generation that grow up in Europe are more literate and educated than their parents that arrived here several years ago, many of them still think imaginatively instead of conceptually, as is expressed in their interest in and use of proverbs and several forms of art. When sharing the Gospel with Muslims we therefore should use imaginary instead of logical concepts and Proverbs provides us with many images of Biblical truth. This might be the reason why Jesus used parables, several of which were closely linked to verses from Proverbs, to communicate truth in the oral culture of His day. We've seen in chapter one that one of the strengths of a proverb is its indirect nature. In Moroccan culture proverbs are used to warn someone or advice him to change his course, to criticize him or to express dissatisfaction with a certain behavior, while at the same time respecting his or her honor. In such a context it makes sense to use Biblical proverbs in order to have someone change his allegiance from Mohammed to Christ.

It Provides Common Ground between God's Truth and their Truth

Many Muslims have a negative view of the Bible, believing its content has been corrupted and falsified and as a result is no longer in agreement with the truth revealed by God as found in the Qur'an. Proverbs with more than 100 verses that are believed to be compatible with the moral values of the Qur'an and hundreds of verses that are similar in content and sometimes in wording to proverbs they are familiar with, might give a Moroccan reading Proverbs a sense of familiarity.

McKenzie believes that the fact that the book of Proverbs contains proverbs that might have originated from secular and neighboring countries "suggests that one homiletical use of proverbs is to single out cultural proverbs which evidence a degree of congruity with aspects of the faith community's worldview, clarifying their theological implications for the faith community by placing them in its theological context."[304]

A Moroccan reading Proverbs will not immediately come across concepts and doctrines that are opposed to his beliefs, like the Jesus being the Son of God or the Trinity, or clear references to Israel. Proverbs presents the world as created by a personal and transcendent God and emphasizes that those who live in right relationship with Him are truly wise and will live forever. Because this is also reflected in the teachings of Islam, the message of Proverbs most likely will appeal to Moroccans.

---

[304] Alyce M. McKenzie, "The preacher as subversive sage: preaching on biblical proverbs," in *Proverbium* (: DeProverbio.com, 1995), 176.

Also the fact that Proverbs bears the name of Solomon contributes might also be appealing to many Muslims, who know about the person of Solomon, who is highly venerated in the Qur'an. Harun Yahya, a Turkish Muslim scholars writes: "Like all other prophets, Prophet Solomon (peace be unto him) invited people to believe in God, avoid associating any other thing or being with Him, and obey His commands and recommendations."[305]

When they begin to see that Proverbs contains many verses that are similar in content and sometimes wording as their own proverbs, Moroccans may realize that Christianity is not as foreign to their culture as they thought.

It Connects the Christian Faith with Daily Life

Many Muslims in Europe have a negative perception of Christianity based on what they've been taught in the mosque, at home or at school. Living in European countries, with churches in almost every village, town and city, they need to see what the relationship is between the Christian faith and the practices and policies in society. They need to know what it means to be a follower of the Father of Jesus Christ.

Proverbs is one of the books in the Bible that seems to be written with this purpose in mind. Beardslee commented: "In the Hebraic and Jewish world wisdom served of building a bridge between the perspective of faith and the experience of men outside the circle of faith."[306]

Despite its universalistic nature and the fact that only 10% of the verses contain direct references to God, the book of Proverbs is religious true and true and clearly integrates theology into daily life.

Often Christians enter into discussions with Muslims focusing on the theological issues that separate the two religions. This often closes the door to a meaningful relationship. While theological differences have to be addresses in the process, it might be far better to start showing them through our own life and from the Bible itself how God's truth is connected to the ordinary life. Proverbs is a great tool for doing so.

---

[305] Harun Yahya, "Prophet Solomon (pbuh)," *Union Of Faiths.com; Muslims, Christians And Jews, Brotherhood Of The Three Religions*, http://www.unionoffaiths.com/article19_1.html. (accessed February 27, 2006).

[306] Beardslee, 162.

Recommendations

Having established that the book of Proverbs is a good tool for sharing God's truth with Muslims in general and Moroccan Muslims in particular, there are some things to keep in mind when using this tool:

The whole Book or Individual Proverbs?

To read consecutively through a series of what seem to be self-contained units in the book of Proverbs is to impose a heavy strain on the mind. The imagination becomes jaded, the memory dazed by the march of too swiftly changing images. Many proverbs, particularly those in chapters 10-29, have little or nothing in common with what precedes or what follows.

Handing our Muslim friend the book of Proverbs might be compared to giving him a box of Belgian chocolates and ask him to eat it all at the same time. The chocolates seem to be best taken one at a time and enough time to digest the one before taking the other and this might be the same for the proverbs in the book of Proverbs.

The proverbs are situation-sensitive that must not be applied mechanically or absolutely. "Their validity depends on the right time and the right circumstance."[307]

Distributing Proverbs as a separate booklet to Muslims that are not familiar with the Bible should be encouraged by all means, but it should be accompanied by an introduction which addresses the question 'are proverbs always true?' and by the advice that often is put on labels coming with medicines: 'take one a day'.

Besides using Proverbs as a separate booklet, there are other ways to use the content of the book, like producing booklets that contain proverbs around the same theme, e.g. 30 proverbs for married couples, 30 proverbs for youth.

Linking Proverbs with Moroccan Proverbs

In chapter three verses from Proverbs were compared with Moroccan proverbs. A lot more could be done in linking, comparing, contrasting Proverbs with Moroccan proverbs. Each Christian who has Moroccan friends could start his or her own collection of Moroccan proverbs and start comparing them with verses from the book of Proverbs. But the book of Proverbs could be used in a valuable way even by those who have no knowledge of Moroccan proverbs. One thing that has become clear in this study that the given the popularity of proverbial use among Moroccans, Christians should use Proverbs more in their conversations

---

[307] Tremper Longman III, 49.

with their Moroccan friends. Arnot points out: "Considering how great a place proverbs hold in human language, and how great a part they act in human life, it was to be expected that the Spirit would use that instrument, among others, in conveying the mind of God to men."[308]

Make the Connection between Woman Wisdom and Jesus Christ

Although Proverbs is an excellent tool to bridge the gap between the truth of the Bible and the worldview and religion of the Moroccans in Europe, we have to keep in mind that it is not the whole Gospel. As Christians we believe that the Person and work of Jesus Christ is central to the Christian faith. The fact is Proverbs does not speak about Him in clear terms. It does not quote His words, says nothing about His life, death and resurrection, which are essential doctrines of the Christian faith. In chapter five it was pointed out that the metaphor of Woman Wisdom, who plays a prominent role in the first nine chapters of Proverbs and in fact provides the hermeneutical grid through which the rest of the book should be read, has several parallels to the person and work of Jesus Christ. But we have to realize that our Muslim friends will not see the link between Woman Wisdom and Jesus Christ without the enlightenment of the Holy Spirit and our help.

It is much like the Ethiopian eunuch in Acts 8:26-40, who read a part of God's word, but wondered who it spoke about. God provided him with a Christian friend (Phillip) who "began with that very passage of Scripture and told him the good news about Jesus" (Acts 8:36). Our Muslim friend needs our help to discover the good news about Jesus in the pages of the book of Proverbs.

Plant the Seeds

"Biblical proverbs … are like seeds clumped together in an unopened packet, which yearn to be poured out in the preacher's palm and sown, along-side their secular counterparts, in the soil of everyday life."[309]

Besides using the book of Proverbs as a separate booklet, we should also look for creative ways to use individual proverbs. Underneath some suggestions:

Use Oroverbs in Personal Conversations

Christians relating to Muslims should familiarize themselves with the proverbs that are used by their friends seek for ways to link them or contrast

---

[308] William Arnot, *Studies in Proverbs* (Grand Rapids: Kregel, 1978), 16, 17.
[309] McKenzie, 175.

them with proverbs from Proverbs. Also, they should learn to purposefully include Proverbs in their conversations and use them at the appropriate time.

Print Proverbs on a Poster

Several years ago a publicity agency, collaborated with Moroccan street youth to print posters with Moroccan proverbs (e.g. *Respect and you will be respected*). The font was a specially designed Dutch character in Arabic style. The posters were placed at strategic places throughout the city of Amsterdam and became quite popular.[310] It would be worthwhile to print posters that have a verse from Proverbs, possibly in connected with a similar Moroccan proverb.

In a Dramatized Format on Television or Video

As mentioned in chapter five, a Christian agency is presently working on producing a series of television programs in which they link Proverbs with popular Egyptian proverbs. This seems an excellent way to use the book of Proverbs and it would be good to produce something similar with the other Islamic cultures in mind and made available on DVD etc.

Organizing a Cultural Event to Share and Compare Proverbs

A cultural organization led by a Moroccan woman, involved in building bridges between different cultures would like to organize an event during which people from different cultures would share and compare popular proverbs.[311] During such an event Christians would be able to share verses from the book of Proverbs.

Through Art

A Dutch artist was asked to make several wall paintings for a multicultural school in the Netherlands. She decided to make something that would incorporate existing Dutch and Turkish and Moroccan proverbs to help the children bridge the cultural gaps.[312] Christian artists find similar ways to build bridges between the book of Proverbs and Moroccan proverbs.

There are many other ways individual verses from Proverbs have been used or could be used e.g. on greeting cards or in electronic signature[313].

---

[310] I collaborated with this publicity agency in ministry with Moroccans in other projects during the period these posters were published.

[311] She expressed this interest in personal conversation in June 2004.

[312] Babette Wagenvoort, "Nieuwe Nederlandse Spreekwoorden,", 2005, www. nieuwenederlandsespreekwoorden.nl/ (accessed February 27, 2006).

[313] Something I have started doing since 6 years.

Christian websites visited by Moroccans could have 'a proverb of the day'. Christian magazines could include a section called 'Wisdom from Above' and print verses from the book of Proverbs. When we are serious of using the seeds of God's truth that the proverbs in the book of Proverbs are, we may find many more creative ways to use them for God's glory and for the salvation of our Moroccan friends.

Concluding Remark

God wants to share His love and truth with the whole world, including our Muslim friends. It is the conclusion of this book that the book of Proverbs is one of the most valuable tools, particularly in combination with local proverbs, to lead our Muslim friends from accepting familiar truth via embracing less familiar truth to worshiping the One who said: I am the truth (John 14:6).

Works Cited

30 Days Global Prayer Network. "Pray For The Kabyles Of Algeria." http://www.30-days.net/email03/day04.htm. (accessed February 23, 2006).

A.S., Christian in Mali. A personal letter to the author. May 6, 2004.

Abdessalami Mubarak. "Moroccan Proverbs." *Abdessalami On Line.* www.angelfire.com/rnb/abdessalami/amthal.html. (accessed February 20, 2006).

Ali, Abdullah Yusuf. *The Holy Qur'an: English Text and Translation.* Kuala Lumpur: Islamic Book Trust, 2003.

Archer, Gleason. *A Survey of OT Introduction.* Chicago: Moody Press, 1994.

Arnot, William. *Studies in Proverbs.* Grand Rapids: Kregel, 1978.

Ask The Econsultant. "Moroccan Proverbs." http://www.econsultant.com/proverbs/moroccan/index.html. (accessed February 20, 2006).

Baardwijk, Corrie, Els Dragt, Allerd Peeters, Paul Vierkant. *Mediagebruik etnische publieksgroepen.* Hilversum: Nederlandse Programma Stichting.

Ball, Lamaan. "What Islam Says About The Bible." *Ask About Islam,* July 6, 2002. www.islamonline.net/servlet/Satellit?pagename=IslamOnline-English-AAbout Is-lam/AskAboutIslamE/AskAboutIslamE&cid=1123996015484/ (accessed February 20, 2006).

Barakat, Halim. *The Arab World: Society, Culture and State.* Berkeley and Los Angeles: University of California Press, 1993.

Barakat, R.A. *A Contextual Study of Arabic Proverbs.* FF Communications, vol. XCVI, no. 226. Helsinki: Suomalainen Tiedeakatemia, 1980.

Beardslee, William. "Uses of the Proverb in the Synoptic Gospel." In *The Wisdom of Many: essays on the proverb,* ed. Wolfgang Mieder & Alan Dundes. New York: Garland, 1981.

Boström, L. *The God of the Sages: The Portrayal of God in the Book of Proverbs.* Stockholm: Almqvist & Wiksell, 1990.

Bousetta, Hassan. "Kunst, cultuur en literatuur in de Marokkaanse gemeenschap in Nederland." *Migrantenstudies* 4 (1996): 182-194.

C.H., Christian worker in Morocco. A personal letter. April 7, 2004.

Creative Proverbs. "Creative Proverbs From Morocco." http://creativeproverbs.com/mo01.htm. (accessed February 2, 2006).

Crenshaw, James L. *Old Testament Wisdom; An Introduction.* London: SCM Press Ltd, 1982.

Dann, Robert. *Pretty as a Moonlit Donkey; a whimsical jaunt down the proverbial byways of Moroccan folklore.* Chester: Jacaranda Books, 2001.

————. *Pretty as a Moonlit Donkey.* Chester: Jacaranda Books, 2001.

Dermot Cox, O.F.M. *Proverbs with an Introduction to Sapiential Books*. Wilmington Delaware: Michael Glazier Inc, 1982.

Dillard, Raymond B. and Tremper Longman III. *An Introduction to the OT*. Michigan: Zondervan Publishing House, 1994.

Dunn, James D.G. *Christology in the Making; A New Testament inquiry into the origins of the doctrine of the incarnation*. Philadelphia: The Westminster Press, 1980.

E.M., A Christian worker in Indonesia. A personal letter to the author. September 14, 2005.

El Aissati, Abder & Yahya E-rramdani. "Berbers in Nederland." *Tawiza*, September 24, 2002. www.Tawiza.nl/content/awid.php?id=205&sid=andra=artikel/ (accessed October 20, 2005).

El Ajjouri, Abdes. A personal letter to the author. February 22, 2005.

English Proverb Album. "Morocco Proverbs." http://www.hometopia.com/proverb/prov1moro.html. (accessed February 20, 2006).

Estes, Daniel J. *New Studies in Biblical Theology*. Edited by D.A. Carson. *Hear, my son; teaching and learning in Proverbs 1-9*. Grand Rapids, Michigan: WmB Eerdmans Publishing Co, 1997.

Falwell, Jerry. *Wisdom for Living*. Wheaton, Illinois: SP Publications Inc, 1984.

Focus On Morocco. "The Land of the Moors." 2005. http://www.focusmm.com/morocco/mo_anamn.htm. (Accessed February 20, 2006).

Fritsch, Charles T. "The Gospel in the Book of Proverbs." *Theology Today*, April, 1950, 169-183.

G.M., Egyptian scriptwriter. A personal letter. December 30, 2005.

Goitein, S.D. "The Present-Day Arabic Proverbs as a Testimony to the Social History of the Middle East." In *S.D. Goitein Studies in Islamic History and Institutions*. Leiden: E.J. Brill, 1966.

Greeson, Kevin. http://www.religionnewsblog.com/ (accessed March 17, 2005).

Hall, Donald W. "Anthropod Proverbs On Morocco.". http://entnemdept.ifas.ufl.edu/proverbs.htm. (accessed January 10, 2006).

———. "Anthropod Proverbs.". http://entnemdept.ifas.ufl.edu/proverbs.htm. (accessed September 21, 2005).

Hargraves, Orin. *Culture Shock! Morocco*. London: Kuperard, 1995.

Idrissi, Khalid Mesbahi. *A sociolinguistic approach to the use of proverbs in Moroccan Arabic*. Fes, Morocco.: by the author, 1983.

International Antioch Ministries. "Press Release." June 14, 2004. http://iam-online.net/Press_release_PDFs/IAMTVrelease_Final.com%20(Read-Only).pdf. (Accessed February 20, 2006).

Jones, Edgar. *Proverbs and Ecclesiastes: Introduction and Commentary*. London: SCM Press, 1961.

Kairos International. "The Wisdom Of God." www.kairos.cc/ (accessed February 20, 2006).

Kidner, Derek. *The Wisdom of Proverbs, Job & Ecclesiastes; An introduction to Wisdom Literature*. Leicester: Inter-Varsity Press, 1985.

L.H.,Christian in Tunisia. A personal letter. February 10, 2004.

Lared Business Network. www.lared.org/ (accessed February 20, 2006).

Leatherwood, Rick. "The Wisdom Of God ... as Revealed In Proverbs." *Kairos International*. http://www.kairos.cc/ (accessed February 28, 2006).

Longman III, Tremper. *How to Read Proverbs*. Leicester: InterVarsity Press, 2002.

Maalof, Tony. *Arabs in the Shadow of Israel*. Grand Rapids: Kregel Publications, 2003.

McKenzie, Alyce M. "The preacher as subversive sage: preaching on biblical proverbs." In *Proverbium*, 169-193: DeProverbio.com, 1995.

Mieder, Wolfgang. "Popular Views Of The Proverb." *Deproverbio.com*, 1999. http://www.deproverbio.com/DPjournal/DP,5,2,99/MIEDER/VIEWS.htm. (accessed February 20, 2006).

———. "Tradition and Innovation: Proverbs in Advertising." *Journal of Popular Culture*, no. 11 (1977): 308-319.

Mohamed Ajouaou. "Bestaat De Nederlandse Gastvrijheid?." *Centrum Voor Islam In Europa (c.i.e.)*, March 24, 2003. http://www.flwi.urgent.be/CIE/majouaou4.htm. (accessed February 20, 2006).

Mubarak, Abdessalami. "Moroccan Proverbs." *Abdessalami On Line*. www.angelfire.com/rnb/abdessalami/amthal.html. (accessed February 23, 2006).

Murphy, Roland E. "Can the Book of Proverbs be a Player in "Biblical Theology"?" *Biblical Theolgy Bulletin*, no. 31 (2001): 4-9.

———. "The Kerygma of the Book of Proverbs." *Interpretation* 20 (1966): 1-14.

Nederlandmarokko2005. "De Joden Van Marokko." 2005. www.marokkonederland2005.nl/ (Accessed February 25, 2006).

Nussbaum, Stan (ed.) *The Wisdom of African Proverbs*. CD-ROM. Colorardo Springs: Global Mapping International, 1998.

One Proverb. "Proverbs From 'moon Over Morocco'." http://www.oneproverb.net/bwfolder/mombw.html. (accessed February 5, 2006).

———. "Proverbs From 'moon Over Morocco'." http://www.oneproverb.net/bwfolder/mombw.html. (accessed February 5, 2006).

Penfield, Joyce and Mary Duru. "Proverbs: Metaphors That Teach." *Anthropological Quarterly* 61, no. 3 (1988): 119-128.

Peterson, Eugene. *The Message*. Colorado Springs: NavPress Publishing Group, 1996.

Phalet, Karen (ed). *Moslim in Nederland*. Den Haag: Sociaal en Cultureel Planbureau.

Phillips, Godfrey E. *The Transmission of the Faith*. London: Lutterworth Library, 1946.

R.D, a Christian worker in Morocco. A personal letter. August 29, 2004.

Ross, Allan P. *The Expositor's Bible Commentary*. Edited by Frank E. Gaebelein. *Volume 5*. Grand Rapids, Michigan: The Zondervan Corporation, 1991.

Sadiqi, Fatima. *Women, Gender and Language in Morocco*. Leiden; Boston: Brill, 2003.

School Zonder Racisme. "Schoolpartnerschappen Vlaanderen Marokko." http://schoolzonderracisme.be/marokko/intercult/marcopolo/marcospreek.htm. (accessed Deceber 21, 2004).

Singh, A. Personal letter on August 21, 2004.

Slack, Jim. "Western Analytical Cultures Vs. Oral Relational Societies." *The Strategic Network*, 2004. http://www.newway.org/strategy_network/western_analytical_vs_oral_cultures.htm. (accessed February 27, 2006).

Steinmann, Andrew E. "Proverbs 1-9 As A Solomonic Composition." *Journal of the Evangelical Theological Society*, no. 43.4 (December 2000): 659-674.

Tawiza Amazigh Startpagina. "Spreekwoorden." http://www.tawiza.nl/content/sectie. php?cid=49&secties=cat/ (accessed February 27, 2006).

Tawiza.nl. "Spreekwoorden." http://tawiza.nl/content/sectie/php?cid=49&secties=cat/ (accessed November 10, 2005).

Taylor, Archer."Wisdom of Many and Wit of One." In *The Wisdom of many: Essays on the proverb*, ed. Wolfgang Mieder & Alan Dundes. New York: Garland, 1981.

Thompson, John Mark. *The Form and Function of Proverbs in Ancient Israel.* The Hague: Mouton and Co. N.V, 1974.

Tuinstra, E.W. *Spreuken I* [Proverbs 1]. Baarn: Callenbach, 1996.

Wagenvoort, Babette. "Ingezonden Spreekwoorden." *Nieuwe Nederlandse Spreekwoorden*, 2005. http://nieuwenederlandsespreekwoorden.nl/index2.html. (accessed February 10, 2006).

————. "Nieuwe Nederlandse Spreekwoorden." . http://www.nieuwenederlands espreekwoorden.nl/index2.html. (accessed November 15, 2005).

Waltke, Bruce K. *The Book of Proverbs, Chapter 1-15.* Grand Rapids: William B. Eerdmans Publishing Company, 2004.

Webster, Sheila K. "Arabic Proverbs and Related Forms." In *Proverbium: Yearbook of International Proverb Scholarship*, 179-194. Burlington, Vermont: University of Vermont, 1986.

Westermarck, Edward. *Wit and Wisdom in Morocco: A Study of Native Proverbs.* New York: Horace Liveright Inc, 1931.

Whybray, R.N. *The Book of Proverbs: A Survey of Modern Study.* Leiden: Brill, 1995.

William A. VanGemeren, ed. *The New International Dictionary of Old Testament Theology and Exegesis.* Vol. 4, *The Topical Dictionary.* Grand Rapids: Zondervan Publishing House, 1997.

Woodcock, Eldon. *Proverbs: A Topical Study.* Grand Rapids, Michigan: Zondervan Publishing House, 1988.

World Of Quotes And Proverbs Archive. "16 Sayings For Moroccan Proverbs." / (accessed January 20, 2006).

World Of Quotes. "16 Sayings For Moroccoan Proverbs." www.worldofquotes.com/proverb/Moroccan/ (accessed January 20, 2006).

Yahya, Harun. "Prophet Solomon (pbuh)." *Union Of Faiths.com; Muslims, Christians And Jews, Brotherhood Of The Three Religions.* http://www.unionoffaiths.com/article19_1.html. (accessed February 27, 2006).

Yassin, Mahmoud Aziz F. "Spoken Arabic Proverbs." *Bulletin of the School of Oriental and African Studies*, no. 51 (1988): 59-68.

Bert de Ruiter

Sharing Lives

Overcoming Our Fear of Islam

This book argues that the single greatest hindrance to Christian witness amongst Muslims in Europe is fear.

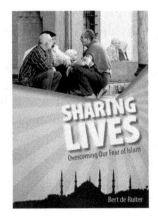

Many European Christians fear that Europe will gradually turn into Eurabia, or Islamic domination of Europe, and they ignore the efforts of Muslims to adapt to the European context, a situation pointing to a future scenario of Euro-Islam, or Islam being Europeanized. The author argues that instead of an attitude of fear, which leads to exclusion, Christians should develop an attitude of grace, which leads to embrace.

After analyzing books and courses developed to help Christians relate to Muslims, he concludes that these mostly concentrate on providing information and skills, instead of dealing with one's attitude. Because of this the author developed a short course to help Christians overcome their fear of Islam and Muslims and to encourage Christians to share their lives with Muslims and to share the truth of the Gospel.

Pb. • XIII + 209 pp. • £ 13.95 • US$ 22.95
ISBN 978-3-941750-22-7

VTR Publications • Gogolstr. 33 • 90475 Nürnberg • Germany
info@vtr-online.eu • http://www.vtr-online.eu

Deborah Meroff

Europe: Restoring Hope

The continent known for over 1000 years as the heartland of Christianity has gone into spiritual arrest. Drawing from the experience of many individuals and organisations, this book takes a hard look at four population groups at the centre of Europe's heart trouble: marginalised people, Muslims, youth and nominal and secular Europeans. Here is proof that it is possible to restore hope to this great continent when God's people work together. This practical resource supplies all the motivation and information we need to get started.

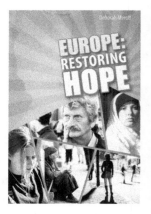

"Europe is very likely a battleground for the future of global Christianity... I hope that whoever reads these pages will be encouraged and inspired to prayer and action."
Jiří Unger
President of the European Evangelical Alliance

"My wife Drena and I have now been based in Europe for 50 years. Debbie Meroff's book True Grit was one of the most important books in our lives, and her new book on Europe is another cutting edge, must-read!"
George Verwer
Founder and International Co-ordinator Emeritus, OM International

"This book shows that God is still at work in Europe. He is building his church despite many challenges. And he wants to see each one of us playing an active part in restoring hope to Europe!"
Frank Hinkelmann
European Director, OM International

Pb. • VIII + 296 pp. • £ 14.95 • US$ 24.95
ISBN 978-3-941750-06-7

VTR Publications • Gogolstr. 33 • 90475 Nürnberg • Germany
info@vtr-online.com • http://www.vtr-online.com

Lightning Source UK Ltd.
Milton Keynes UK
UKHW010707160223
417123UK00005B/524